MW01154609

THE JEWEL TEA COMPANY

ITS HISTORY AND PRODUCTS

C.L. Miller

Schiffer Publishing Ltd

77 Lower Valley Road, Atglen, PA 19310

DEDICATION

To Evelyn L. Grider Miller, Lillie M. Sollars Miller, Rosa Anna Kelley Grider, women who I observed shop the Jewel way and Mary Reed "Mary Dunbar" Hartson, and all of those Mrs. Brown's.

Copyright © 1994 by C.L. Miller
Library of Congress Catalog Number: 94-65854

All rights reserved. No part of this work may be reproduced or used in any forms or by any means–graphic, electronic or mechanical, including photocopying or information storage and retrieval systems–without written permission from the copyright holder.

Printed in China
ISBN: 0-88740-634-3

Published by Schiffer Publishing, Ltd.
77 Lower Valley Road
Atglen, PA 19310
Please write for a free catalog.
This book may be purchased from the publisher.
Please include $2.95 postage.
Try your bookstore first.

We are interested in hearing from authors
with book ideas on related subjects.

In 1916 the above "Diamond JTC Trade Mark" appeared in a magazine for Jewel employees. This Diamond logo can be seen on various Jewel products along with "SKI-RO BRAND" wording. The re-designed packaging from that era was to commemorate the event when the Jewel Tea Company was incorporated under the laws of New York. Instead of "JEWEL" the brand name became "SKI-RO" after Frank Skiff and Frank Ross. This logo was in effect until approximately 1919, when Mr. Skiff retired as President of the company. The "Diamond JTC Trade Mark" can be found alone on various items.

ACKNOWLEDGEMENTS

Without the assistance, knowledge, and support of many collectors of this famous Hall China this book would have never been possible. I can never tell you how much I appreciate everyone who opened their homes, basements, garages, and storage units to share their collection's.

I must publicly acknowledge the full endorsement of former N.A.L.C.C. President Suzan Fausset, various club members, friends, and family.

From over 320 letters mailed out. Suzan was among the first to contact me after receiving my letter of introduction. Her exceptional Non-Hall Autumn Leaf collection which she so graciously photographed in her Oklahoma home was the first series of over 100 photographs I received. Through her full patronage in my project she led me to collectors across the United States. Word soon spread and in turn many collectors called me personally or wrote. I appreciate all those letters of support. Many times Suzan lifted my spirits when I felt destitute and came to my defense.

Patti Byerly, Ohio Director and Coordinator of her own Autumn Leaf Show, and her husband Neal opened their home for photographing their extensive collection on four consecutive Sunday's. Patti was the gracious hostess who had prepared ice tea in an original "Solar Jewel Tea Jar." Patti without a second thought loaned her extensive collection of Jewel Home Shopping Service catalogues and various documents for my research. Whenever I had a question, Patti always would advise me or direct me to a reliable source.

When I arrived in Barrington, Illinois, former N.A.L.C.C. President Shirley Easley graciously opened her home, introduced her family, and was a delightful hostess, guide and adviser during my stay in the area. Shirley was so thoughtful when she mailed her collection of 1946 Jewel News, and other documents, for my examination and use in word or photograph.

President Michael Williams and Mr. Matt McManaman of the J.T. Merchandise Services, Inc., Barrington, Illinois for allowing me access to the Jewel Archives. President John Thompson and Mr. Everson Hall of The Hall China Company. President David Dunn, Commercial Decal of Ohio and the Jewel Food Stores, for their cooperation. Mrs. Eva Zeisel for her correspondence and endorsement. I appreciate all of you.

The gracious hospitality that was extended in the Michigan home of Bill and NanSue Hamilton, when I arrived to photograph their extension collection. The Hamilton's are the most pleasant, caring people I have met in a long time. They are quite knowledgeable of their extensive collection. NanSue had prepared an exceptional dinner for myself, the Byerly's and Richard Schwartz, who so kindly met us and brought many of his salesman awards, so that I might also photograph them.

Later that day we drove to Richard's home to photograph his Jewel products. Richard, Bill and NanSue fully endorsed this major project and I appreciate their advice, letters, phone calls, photographs and the numerous documents they graciously provided me.

Ohio residents Bill and Dee Hedges for allowing me to photograph their large collection on a sultry Sunday afternoon. These fine people I had met a number of years ago at a local antique show and a friendship soon developed. They introduced me to the N.A.L.C.C. organization and have supported me during these past two years.

Florida resident Opal Hancock who believed in me and this major project I had undertaken. This delightful woman without demur mailed many packages to my home for research and never set a limit for there return. She phoned numerous times to check on my progress and offered her assistance and gave me encouragement. Any item related to Jewel, if Opal had it, was available for my research without ever asking. We were very fortunate that only one piece of china was damaged.

Friends, Cindy and Mike Schneider, I could never say enough about these fine people. Sometime ago I approached this well known writer about doing a book on the Jewel Tea Co. Mike at the time had contracts and deadlines to meet of his own. Later as a guest in my home, Mike encouraged me to write the book. After some time of serious consideration, I accepted the challenge. At that time the wheel's were put into motion and I was introduced to Schiffer Publishing Co., and later to Jeff Snyder who was to be my editor. Mike and Cindy offered professional advice and gave their faithful support, and I appreciate both of them.

China Specialties, Inc., President Virginia Wilson, Joel Wilson and their staff, for the full support and endorsement of this publication and their kind consideration in offering a special commemorative Hall Autumn Leaf piece in connection with the publication release of this book and the celebration of the 60th anniversary of Autumn Leaf China.

I am so grateful for the support and dedication of each of you. If I have overlooked anyone, I am truly sorry. I wish to thank each of you from the bottom of my heart for making this possible.

Al Barnes, Fred Beghul, Margaret and Doug Belmonte, Thelma Blow, Elizabeth J. and Charles Boyce, Joan Brinkman, Nancy Brock, Norma and Bernie Brush, Author and Columnist - Tad Burness, Char and Dan Casey, Cascade, Iowa Public Library, Betty Carson, Columbus, Ohio Public Library, Sue and Dave Cross, Timothy Cromwell, Sharon Costanza, Author and Columnist - Jo Cunningham, Joyce and Don DeJong, Doug B. Dupler who provided the transportation, ran numerous errands, assisted in the labeling and recording of over 1600 photographs.

Sandra Hooper Edwards, Donald P. Hammond, James Howard Hooper, Sr., Nita and Jim Kinder, Julie Kuhse, Harriet Kurshadt, Lynda and Lon Lemons, Laurel and Mike Long, Karen and Rick Marshall, Wayne McCarthy, Dave and Sue McDiarmid, Annie Mercer, and Maureen Moos for their encouragement during the past two years.

To Megan Moos who kindly mailed a Christmas gift to my home. Megan gave me her original J.T.'s General Store teddy bear that she had outgrown, with the understanding, I was to give the bear a lot of T.L.C. I appreciate her kindness and thoughtfulness.

Bonnie Nemluvil, Oak Park, Illinois Public Library, Artist - Ruth Ohlinger, Ollys and Paul H. Preo, Harry and Judy Pomroy, Pansy C. Ramsey, Lorraine Zeno Rippey, Bernetta and Larry Scott, Richard C. Schwartz, Emery E. Seider, Norma Jones-Shaughnessy, Connie and Carl Sipes, Illustrations - Bob Stokes, June and Randell Weales, Jackie Weiner, James Woodruff, Grace Zeno, Janey and Herb Zollinger. To my family and friends who supported and encouraged me these past two years and all of the Mrs. Brown's who traded the Jewel way and to those collector's who wish to remain anonymous.

In 1933 the above "Barrington Circle Logo" appeared on many products. Many of these products also will be marked 1933. In one of the outer circles appears "Reg. U.S. Pat. Off", inside the larger circle "TESTED AND APPROVED BY MARY DUNBAR - JEWEL HOME-MAKERS INSTITUTE". The center section of the logo is the 1922 style "JEWEL T". Products can be found marked 1933 with the same logo, but excluding the wording. It is wise to remember that Jewel moved into their new headquarters in Barrington, Illinois in April 1930. Whereas, we see the words "JEWEL PARK" on many products.

CONTENTS

Introduction 7

Chapter 1. Jewel Products 9
  Condition Factors 9
  With A Guarantee 9
  Old Mother Hubbard 9
  The Jewel Guarantee 10
  Baking and Spices 10
  Coffee Cake Mix 22
  Jewel Extracts 23
  Breakfast Products 24
  Coffee, Tea and Cocoa Products 27
  Cleaners, Soaps and Beauty Products 40
  Snacks, Jello and Treats 54
  Jewel Macaroni, Spaghetti, Noodles 58
  City Postman 64

Chapter 2. Autumn Leaf Kitchenware
      and Dinnerware 65
  Condition Factor 65
  Three-Piece Utility Bowl Set 66
  Cake Plate and Candy Dish 68
  Metal Base Candleholders 70
  Covered Casserole 71
  Custard Cups 72
  Cookie Jars 73
  Beverage Pitcher 74
  Open Stock 76
  Gravy Boat 76
  Marmalade and Mustard 77
  Plates 77
  Platters 80
  Fruit and Cereal Bowls 81
  Serving Bowls 82
  Utility Pitcher 85
  Soups Bowls 86
  Stack Set 88
  Range Set 89

Salt and Pepper Shakers 89
Souffle (French Baker) Dishes 90
2-Pint French Baker 90
Individual Souffle 90
Fort Pitt 92
Oval and Round Warmer 93
Tidbit Trays 95
Bean Pots 97
Butter Dishes 100
Vases 106
Buyer Beware 107
Barrington Archives 112

Chapter 3. The Breakfast Set 114
  Table Service 114
  Jewel Service, 1936 Tempo 115
  Jewel Meets Demand 115
  Quality and Distinction 115
  Jewel Service 115
  600 Hall Workers 115

Chapter 4. World War II 116
  Vivid Memories 116
  Daily Abuse 117
  Wooden 117
  Tinware 118
  Canister Sets 118
  Cake Safe 119
  Autumn Leaf Metal Chair 120
  Autumn Leaf Cleaner Can 122
  Flour Sifters 123
  Picnic Thermos 124
  Trays 126
  Wastebaskets 127
  Coaster Set 127
  Hot Pads 129
  Tins 132
  Comb Case 137

Chapter 5. Cookware 138
  A Variety of Cookware 138
  Mary Dunbar Heat-Flow Ovenware 140
  Mary Dunbar Frypan 142
  Royal Glas-Bake 143
  Porcelain-Clad Cookware 143
  Club Aluminum Hammercraft 149

Chapter 6. NonHall Autumn Leaf 152
  Paden 152
  Crooksville 159
  Vernon Kilns 164
  Columbia 166
  Limoges 172
  Crown 175
  Unmarked Autumn Leaf 176
  Japanese Autumn Leaf 179

Chapter 7. Coffee and Teapots 181
  The Story of Jewel Coffee From
    The Plantation To Your Cup 182
  Jewel Coffee 183
  The Coffee Expert 185
  Improved 8-Cup Coffee Maker
    Introduced 187
  Variations 187
  Granulators 187
  Coffee & Teapots 189
  Sugar and Creamer 197
  Cups and Saucers 198
  Jewel's Private Collection 200
  Canisters 200
  Autumn Leaf Canister Set 201
  Square Canister Set 201
  Coopertone Canister Set 202

Jewel Coffee Urn and Mugs 203
Commentary Mugs 204
Coffee Advertisements 204

Chapter 8. Cameo Rose 205

Chapter 9. N.A.L.C.C. 219
  A Special Announcement 219
  Club Pieces 219
  Complimentary Gifts 230

Chapter 10. China Specialties 231

Chapter 11. Autumn Leaf Ceramics 243
  Carolyn Robbins 243
  Connie Sipes 246
  Dianne Daves 249
  Unknown 250

Chapter 12. Haviland 251
  The Queen of China 251
  Haviland by W.D. Smith, Secretary—
    1927 Jewel 251
  Genuine Autumn Leaf Haviland 251

Appendix I 257
Appendix II 258
Appendix III 259
Appendiix IV 260
Appendix V 261
Appendix VI 262
Bibliography 263
Index 264
Price Guide 267

Shown above, what I refer to as the Melior/Helvetical "JEWEL HOME SHOPPING SERVICE" logo, era 1960-1966. Melior/Helvetical refers to the style of print.

6

INTRODUCTION

It is my pleasure to provide you with "The Jewel Tea Company. It's History and Products" after almost two years of research. It is impossible to photograph and list every item provided by this historical company. Many items are unaccountable, many are lost to time. Jewel premiums were only sold or given by home delivery to their customers. New items were add regularly and offered to Mrs. Brown as premiums for the purchase of Jewel products. Items not popular with customers were short-lived and are difficult for the collector to find. Many of the dates cannot be ascertain.

Mrs. Brown was a general title name given by the Jewel Tea organization and salesmen when they referred to Jewel's women customers in general. Today the title of Mrs. Brown reflects those dedicated women who shopped the Jewel way.

I have tried to provide a wide variety of products, as each collector is different. Numerous photographs have been taken or supplied by various collectors. The Jewel Tea Company had many items that were considered premium items over the years. Some were exclusive and others were available from other sources.

If I have made mistakes or misled anyone, I am truly sorry and apologize for this. Every Jewel booklet, brochure, Jewel News or Catalog was not available for my research.

While beginning in 1899, the company was in business under the Jewel name from 1901 until 1981. In 1981 the firm gave up any rights to the Jewel name when the parent corporation, Jewel Companies, Inc., allowed the old Jewel Tea Company to become a cooperative.

Around the turn of the twentieth century, one would purchase coffee from bins or large tin canisters from the local grocery store. The coffee may have been out of the roaster for weeks or even months, affecting the quality and freshness.

Frank Vernon Skiff was a young solicitor for the India Tea Company in Chicago when he set up his own tea wagon operation in 1899. With a horse and wagon, $700 and an idea, Mr. Skiff planned to operate a door-to-door route to regular customers, selling them fresh coffee from the roaster. His idea was to call on them every week on the same day and approximately the same hour. A marked improvement over grocery store coffee. Mr. Skiff also carried spices, tea and other grocery items and quickly developed a following.

Frank Skiff was joined in 1901 by his brother-in-law, Frank P. Ross. Mr. Ross was to secure new customers for the growing business. Mr. Skiff was quiet with a wry sense of humor while Mr. Ross was an energetic extrovert; both men worked well together in forming the company in those early days. They settled on the "Jewel Tea Company" name in 1901; the name "Jewel" being understood as the name for anything special, be it a thing or an idea.

In 1903, Jewel Tea was incorporated in Illinois and acquired a three-story building, substantially larger than their first establishment, for roasting their own coffee. By 1906, the company had it's own manufacturing equipment and was producing the first products under their own label, including baking powder and extract.

In 1914, Jewel Tea allocated profit sharing credits for groceries purchased as a cash credit to the customer's premium account balance. In 1923 Mrs. Mary Reed Hartson was hired to head a quality control staff for the Home Service Division, the forerunner of the Homemakers' Institute. In 1924, the Homemakers' Institute was launched with a new concept that linked customers with the Jewel headquarters where they tested recipes, developed new ones, and where household ideas were collected and published in the Jewel News.

In 1925, another form of service was offered the customer. Anyone with a question or suggestion on "home cookery" could write a woman in the company dubbed the "Jewel Lady." A response would be forthcoming. Two years later, the Jewel Lady was personalized, introducing herself to the public. She decided to use her maiden name, Mary Dunbar, rather than her married name, Mrs. Mary Reed Hartson.

One of the most important decisions Hall China has ever made was that of entering into an agreement with The Jewel Tea Company to produce the famous Autumn Leaf Pattern, which you will see continuously throughout this book. The Hall China connection dates back to the mid-1920s when Jewel offered Hall teapots as premiums.

Exclusively made by the Hall China Company of East Liverpool, Ohio for the "Jewel Home Shopping Service", the Autumn pattern china could only be purchased through an authorized Jewel Salesman. Jewel acquired the exclusive rights to the famous Autumn Leaf pattern. The Autumn Leaf motif pieces carry a gold backstamp that indicates information pertaining to the manufacture, including the number of the mold and the number of the worker/employee who handled the piece.

On June 27, 1929, Jewel officially broke ground and then, nine months later, completed the Barrington, Illinois building 38 miles northwest of Chicago. This building became their new General Headquarters Office and Midwest Plant in 1930. This well-known structure has undergone many additions since.

The above "Jewel T Scale" logo was introduced in the late teens.

Jewel Companies, Inc. announced their intention on January 29, 1981 to discontinue ownership of the Jewel Home Shopping Service. They planned to transfer the assets to a cooperative organization which would be formed and managed by certain Jewel employees. The Company successfully completed the operation and on May 23, 1981, it was incorporated under the name IHSS, Inc. with J.T.'s General Store as it's trade name (a division of J.T. Merchandise Services).

Many of the words you are about to read are actual Jewel words, either written or spoken by a Jewel official or employee. I feel that their own words provide a better insight into the Jewel operation and the Company. You will be introduced to many symbols which were part of this organization, as well as an array of horses, mules, wagons, carts and trucks.

I hope you will be intrigued by actual historical photographs from the Barrington, Illinois archives and original advertisements reprinted from old issues of the Jewel News, with original captions of premiums and products that were offered.

One of the hardest decisions I had to make was that of cutting apart some of my old Jewel News, those of the late 1920s and early 1930s. During the past two years I had carefully turned each of the brittle pages and watched in shock when they crumbled in my hands. Those pieces of historical paper held a great deal of Jewel's history. Time has taken it's toll and I watched those documents fall apart. I decided then to allow them to continue on in this publication and I carefully began to cut and salvage as much as possible. Many of those pieces of vital information appear in this publication in their entirety, just as they appeared in those disintegrating documents that once laid crumbling in my lap.

Experience the smell of Jewel vanilla and soap products being tested in Jewel Laboratories, as they are introduced to you in their own section, the "Products Chapter." Numerous items or products may be repeated periodically in this publication in order to give you a better understanding.

Meet two women whose dedicated work built an organization of approximately 4000 members across the United States when they formed the National Autumn Leaf Collectors' Club (N.A.L.C.C.).

Prior to Jewel's introduction of the Autumn Leaf pattern, other companies produced the Autumn Leaf motif on their own china lines. You will be amazed at the bold and vivid coloring produced by companies like Paden, Crooksville, Vernon Kilns, Columbia, Limoges, Crown and an unknown Japanese Company.

Inside a Jewel Home you will see how Jewel helped decorate rooms, gave advice on food, on clothing, and offered advice in "Cookware" and "Cameo Rose".

Take part in the flight and destruction of the Hindenburg, and the outbreak of World War II, when metal products ceased to be made. Today Jewel metal items are highly sought after and can be extremely expensive.

Discover Autumn Leaf pieces never offered before through the Jewel Tea Co. when you are introduced to "China Specialties". These pieces are worthy of inclusion in any collection.

You will appreciate the creation of "Autumn Leaf Ceramic" pieces, produced by talented young artists from across the country, and will look at a few of these exceptional pieces which are in big demand in today's market.

"From your parents you learn love and laughter and how to put one foot before the other. But when books are opened you discover that you have wings." — Unknown.

May this book provide you with wings to discover the World of Autumn Leaf, historical data, and the understanding of how important it is to preserve history for future generations.

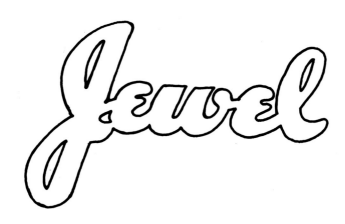

The above "Scripted Jewel" logo was popular during the 1950s - 1960s era. As well as a 1950s era slogan "A Better Place to Work, A Better Place to Trade".

CHAPTER 1
JEWEL PRODUCTS

During Jewel's 75th Anniversary Year, the Jewel Tea Company pointed out that it had been said that Jewel owes it's very existence to the quality and public acceptance of it's grocery products. Jewel manufactured some of their grocery products and it's standard of excellence was unparalleled.

Jewel sold grocery products that homemakers used on a regular basis so that they had a continuing need for them. Around 1930 there were over 300 items in the Jewel line, consisting of coffees, teas, jams and jellies, cake mixes, laundry and cleanings aids, and a line of cosmetic items. This number would drastically increase over the years. It is impossible to show or list every products that Jewel offered. If dates were available I have included them.

The Jewel Tea Company offered their customers premiums as an incentive to buy Jewel products. Products were purchased quickly in order to obtain the premiums while still available. Many collectors of the famous Jewel Tea China are collectors of Jewel cardboard and tins products. Many of the products are shown in several different views.

Condition Factor

Products in mint condition are those free from rust, scratches, or dents and which still retaining their original wrappers. Mint condition products demand higher prices than those in fair to poor condition. Full containers are in high pursuit and demand more than those containers that are empty.

Those products from the early era of Jewel Tea are highly sought after. Sometimes the condition factor does play an important part with these early products. I have seen early Jewel products in poor condition demand higher prices than those of later years.

The outward aspect of a Jewel cardboard container, one that is crushed, torn or ragged in appearance hinders the price, in much the same way as those of metal or tin products.

It is wise to look a container over carefully. With Jewel, as with other companies, "Distributed by" means that someone else manufactured this product. Whereas "Manufactured by" indicates that the product was produced by Jewel.

With A Guarantee

Jewel products, premiums and service were all backed by their unlimited guarantee—satisfaction or your money back.

Customer's dissatisfied with any grocery item was given credit for the amount of the item that she purchased. If she desired, her money was refunded, the item was exchanged, or she was given credit towards another purchase. The salesman showed the credit for a return on a Jewel form, her housecard, and completed an adjustment form.

Old Mother Hubbard

How many times have you repeated to yourself the childhood nursery rhyme "Old Mother Hubbard went to the cupboard"!

According to Mary Dunbar in 1927, when "Mother Hubbard" got there nothing was bare because Mother Hubbard was a smart shopper. When the Coffee-Brown Jewel car stop at the curb in front of her home, Mother Hubbard relied on Jewel for her pantry service needs and her pantry had a variety of each delicacy a-plenty.

A 1927 issue of The Jewel News featured a large selection of Jewel spices — black pepper for utility and general seasoning, for meat dishes, mustard was offered. Mother Hubbard could take her choice of cinnamon, allspice, ginger, and nutmeg for the finer cakes and pastries that she prepared.

She could not find a more complete line of tasty spices than those from Jewel. They were ahead of the household needs, for each package, whether opened or closed, held its strength indefinitely.

When "Old Mother Hubbard" went to her cupboard, the shelves were stocked with Jewel Nutmeg, Allspice, Mustard, Ginger, Black Pepper, and Cinnamon.

There was more than one selection of Jewel Coffee or Jewel Tea. Both were offered in two sizes. Mother Hubbard could indulge her discriminating taste with an array of tea in many sized packages: Orange Pekoe and Pekoe, Imperial Gunpowder, Pan-Fired, Basket-Fired, Ceylon-India, Oolong and Gunpowder, or choose from black, green and mixed teas.

For the general products, there were liquid extracts, spices, toilet articles and soaps. All it took was for her to become acquainted with every Jewel family product by buying them all. Stocking her shelves and using Jewel products in all ways, Mother Hubbard would always be pleased.

In the end no cupboard was bare if you allowed Jewel Tea into your home, as "Old Mother Hubbard" did!

The Jewel Guarantee

In 1969 the question was asked, "Who stood behind the Jewel guarantee for the grocery products that carried the Mary Dunbar seal of approval?"

It was the people, some who were chemists and food technicians, who maintained the high standards of quality control. These people tested the products that Jewel sold and the ingredients which they used in their manufacture.

Once several experimental formulas or recipes were produced, they were then sent to The Homemakers' Institute for evaluation. If it was a baking mix, the technicians baked it; if it was a laundry product, they used it while washing. Through testing like this, technicians were able to find the formula which gave the customer the best performance.

As all grocery items were not manufactured in Barrington, Jewel buyers purchased some of them from outside sources. Those items, as with those actually manufactured in Barrington, were produced to exacting specifications set up by Jewel and were subjected to the careful testing that was used on other Jewel grocery items.

Any product underwent extensive quality testing. Tests were made to determine shelf life—how long a product could be stored and still remained fresh and usable. It might be heated, frozen, and thawed to determine what precautions must be taken in shipping and storage. Products were exposed to sunlight and ultraviolet light to ensure that they would not deteriorate under these conditions. Products were given containers which kept them fresh, potent and dispensable.

A product was then tested by panels of employees and homemakers. If it earned their approval, it was ready for a pilot and/or test run. During the test run, the product was actually manufactured. It was checked every step of the way to determine whether the product could be mixed, filled, and packaged properly.

The Homemakers' Institute Staff made sure that every grocery product delivered the performance, quality and value that the customer demanded. How did the staff know what the customer wanted? They were homemakers, just like the customers they served.

To earn the Homemakers' Seal of Approval, there were five tests every Jewel baking mix had to pass.

In the Barrington laboratory all ingredients were checked to make sure they met Jewel's quality specifications.

Perishable ingredients were checked again when they were ready to be mixed to ensure that they retained the highest purity and freshness.

When a batch was mixed, and before it was packaged, two samples were taken. The laboratory tests one, the other was prepared in the test kitchen. The samples were examined for how well they baked, and for flavor, color, texture, and body.

If the batch tested well, packaging was started. Every half hour one package was taken off the production line and again tested by the Homemakers' Staff.

Each box was checked for proper weight and double sealed to keep freshness in.

Each box or the entire batch was rejected if it failed any one of the tests. Only those mixes which passed all five tests were awarded the seal: TESTED AND APPROVED BY MARY DUNBAR JEWEL HOMEMAKERS INSTITUTE.

Baking and Spices Products

"Melt-in-Your-Mouth" Biscuits

are easy to make with Jewel Baking Powder, for it has double leavening power. That means it "works" both in the dough, before it is placed in the oven, and continues "working" after it is in the oven. It is inexpensive because, on the average, only one teaspoon to a cup of flour is needed. It makes uniform bakings. Made of absolutely pure ingredients. 1-pound can.

The above original advertisement and caption for Jewel Baking Powder appeared in a Jewel News in 1927.

The above original promotion photograph was taken in 1938.

The two pictures, shown above, contained the secret of baking success — Jewel Baking Powder acted twice, once with in contact with liquids and a second time with the application of heat. This double leavening action insured lighter textured cakes and biscuits. Double action permitted the storing of the batter overnight in the ice box/refrigerator, without endangering baking success.

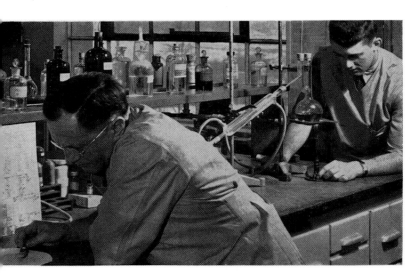

The action of Jewel Baking Powder is tested in the Jewel laboratory in the picture above, dated from the late 1930s.

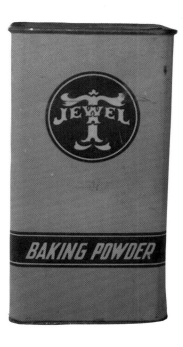

The above exceptional 1-lb. Jewel Baking Powder tin bears the "Jewel T Scale" logo introduced in the late teens. Manufactured by Jewel Tea Co., Chicago, Ill. *Nemluvil Collection.*

The above 1-lb. can of continuous action Jewel Baking Powder was manufactured by Jewel Tea Co., Inc. Jewel Park Barrington, Ill. *Byerly Collection.*

The above glass jar of 1-lb. Jewel Baking Powder is missing it's lid. Manufactured by Jewel Tea Co., Inc., Jewel Park, Barrington, Ill. This baking powder appeared in a promotional photograph in 1946, along with numerous other Jewel products. It is useful to note that if a product is marked Jewel Park, this indicates a date after 1930 when Jewel moved into their Barrington Jewel Park headquarters. *Byerly Collection.*

A different design appears on the above Jewel Tea continuous action Baking Powder. Manufactured by Jewel Tea Co., Inc., Jewel Park, Barrington, Ill. *Byerly Collection.*

Jewel Home Shopping Service Baking Powder, shown above. This can held 16 oz. (one pound) of continuous action baking powder. *Randall Collection.*

Jewel Home Shopping Service, Baking Powder, shown above, 1950s - 1960s. Manufactured by Jewel Tea Co., Inc., Jewel Park, Barrington, Ill. Note the two different forms of Jewel in the above photograph and this photograph. *Byerly Collection.*

You Use It Every Day

JEWEL PEPPER

Since pepper is used for seasoning practically every day, we must be sure of its quality. Jewel Pepper is ground to retain the flavor and conserve the oils. It will not make you sneeze.

5-oz. can.............**35c**

(Profit Sharing Credit 5c.)

Um-m-m! I Smell Cinnamon

JEWEL CINNAMON

What delectable goodies mother makes when she takes the cinnamon can from the shelf. We can hardly wait until they come out of the oven. Kiddies adore that spicy cinnamon flavor and it pleases grown-ups as well. Jewel Cinnamon is a real quality product, convenient and handy to use.

5-oz. can.....**30c**

(Profit Sharing Credit 5c.)

The above brightly colored 5-oz. Jewel Cinnamon tin has had some wear. Jewel Tea Co., Inc., New York - Chicago. *Byerly Collection.*

The above original advertisement and captions for Jewel Black Pepper and Jewel Cinnamon appeared in a 1929 Jewel News.

For That Different Flavor

JEWEL GINGER

A dash of ginger gives that unusual flavor that makes an ordinary dish distinctive. Use it in the syrup poured over canned fruits, or try a little in the water when boiling a fowl. The flavor it gives is delicious.

5-oz. can.............**35c**

(Profit Sharing Credit 5c.)

If You Like Mustard

JEWEL GROUND MUSTARD

Try Jewel Ground Mustard for varying the flavor of your favorite dishes. It has that rich, genuine mustard flavor —snappy and pungent; is made from a selected stock and is absolutely pure.

5-oz. can.....**35c**

(Profit Sharing Credit 5c.)

The above original advertisement and captions for Jewel Ginger and Jewel Mustard appeared in a 1929 Jewel News.

The above 5-oz. Jewel Ginger tin is in near mint condition. Jewel Tea Co., Inc., New York - Chicago. *Byerly Collection.*

The above display of Jewel ginger, nutmeg, and ground mustard were packed by Jewel Tea Co., Inc., Jewel Park, Barrington, Ill. *Byerly Collection.*

Packed by Jewel Tea Co., Inc., Jewel Park, Barrington, Ill., the above Jewel Ginger tin still has the original wrapping. *Byerly Collection.*

The above exceptional 5-oz. 4" tall tin held Jewel Black Pepper. Packed by Jewel Tea Co., Inc., Jewel Park, Barrington, Ill. *Nemluvil Collection.*

The above 5-oz. 4" tall tin held Jewel Ground Mustard. Packed by Jewel Tea Co., Inc., Jewel Park, Barrington, Ill. *Nemluvil Collection.*

The three Jewel spices shown on the right; cinnamon, ginger and all-spice bear the "Jewel T Scale" logo of the late teens. Each tin is marked Jewel Tea Co., Inc., New York - Chicago. *Hedges Collection.*

The above unusual 2-oz. spice tins held ginger and nutmeg. Distributed by Jewel Tea Co., Inc., Barrington, Ill. *Hedges Collection.*

Shown above, "SKI-RO" brand ground ginger. Put up by Jewel Tea Co. Inc. Headquarters, New York - New Orleans - Chicago - San Francisco. "SKI-RO" stands for SKIff-ROss, after Skiff and Ross. This logo was popular from 1916 - 1919 as well as the diamond logo used sometime during 1919. *Preo Collection.*

Shown above, the diamond logo that appears on the back of the opposite carton of ground ginger. This is an exceptional example of this logo. *Preo Collection.*

Shown above, a colorful tin of "SKI-RO" brand spice cloves. Jewel Tea Co. Inc. Headquarters, New York - New Orleans - Chicago - San Francisco appear on this tin. *Busch Collection.*

Shown above, 5 oz. Jewel Black Pepper. Jewel Tea Co., Inc., Jewel Park, Barrington, Ill. *Byerly Collection.*

Shown above in the original wrapper is a 5-oz. Jewel nutmeg. Jewel Tea Co., Inc., Jewel Park, Barrington, Ill. *Byerly Collection.*

Shown above is 5-oz. of Jewel Cinnamon. Jewel Tea Co., Inc., Jewel Park, Barrington, Ill. *Byerly Collection.*

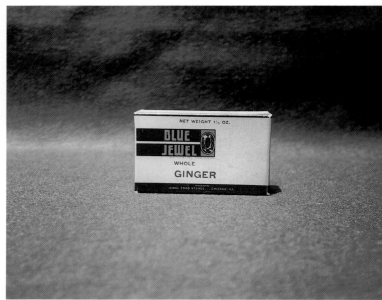

1-1/2 oz. Blue Jewel whole ginger, shown above, 1932©. Distributed by Jewel Food Stores ... Chicago, Ill. *Byerly Collection.*

Shown above, 1-oz. tin of Blue Jewel Ground Cinnamon. A 1932© date appears on the front of this tin. Distributed by Jewel Food Stores ... Chicago, Ill. *Byerly Collection.*

1 oz. Blue Jewel whole cloves, shown above. Distributed by Jewel Food Stores ... Chicago, Ill. *Byerly Collection.*

Jewel Black Ground Pepper, 4" tall, 4 oz. Packed by Jewel Tea Co., Inc., Barrington, Ill. *Nemluvil Collection.*

4 oz. Jewel Ground Black Pepper, shown above. Distributed by Jewel Companies, Inc., Barrington, Ill. 60010. *Blow Collection.*

Shown above, Quick Chef 3-1/4 oz. Chili Powder and a 3 oz. Ground Cinnamon. *Byerly Collection.*

Shown above, 18 oz. Quick Chef carrot cake mix. Note St. Denis cup and saucer and metal base cake stand. *Byerly Collection.*

Pieces of Autumn Leaf china appeared on the covering of the above 15 oz. Quick Chef chocolate fudge n' chips cake mix. *Byerly Collection.*

Italian Style Jewel grated cheese is shown above. *Hedges Collection.*

Coffee Cake Mix

In Jewel's Food Laboratory and Homemakers' Institute in 1946, technicians were working on a Coffee Cake Mix for their customers. When Jewel's food experts were convinced that Jewel Coffee Cake Mix tasted like the real homemade kind, the Jewel Man would begin carrying it.

The new Coffee Cake Mix was to be another add-sugar mix that saved flour and shortening.

In 1925, the above original advertisement and captions appeared in a Jewel News for Lemon Extract and Vanilla Extract.

Jewel brand food coloring "Yellow". Note the "Bar 'N Circle" logo used from 1903 - 1910. Manufactured by Jewel Tea Co., Chicago. *Byerly Collection.*

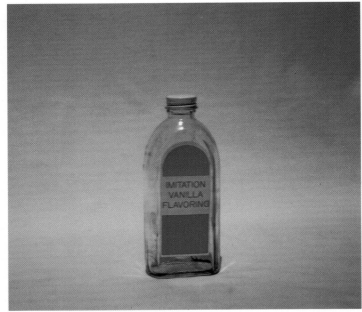

6-drams of Jewel brand non-alcoholic concentrated lemon flavor, priced at 30¢ with the Profit Sharing Plan. Jewel Tea Co., Headquarters, New York - Chicago - New Orleans - San Francisco. *Hedges Collection.*

6 fl. oz. of Jewel Imitation Vanilla flavoring shown above. Manufactured by Jewel Companies Inc., Barrington, Ill 60010. *Lemons Collection.*

Jewel Extracts

In 1938 the machines that filled and capped bottle's of Jewel extracts were almost human. These machines were developed by Jewel's staff of experts.

The operations of bottling Jewel extracts were clean and sanitary as shown in the photograph above. A Jewel employee prepares empty bottle for filling.

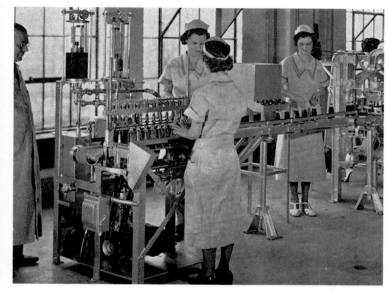

In the photograph above, Jewel staff expert Frank Farwell (extreme left) inspects his machinery. Jewel employees are Adeline Buryanek, Eleanore Meister, Virginia Benson and Margaret Williams.

Frank Farwell, production foreman, Henry Dreckman and Waldo Shuett received the credit for this big step in bottling equipment. The plans developed in the office of Plant Superintendent E.J. Courrier, with the actual construction pieced in between regular jobs and after closing time.

Standard equipment on the market then, performing the same task as this machine, would have cost approximately $9,000. Jewel's machine cost was less than $400 and increased production by 50 percent. The machine was simply constructed so that maintenance costs were also lower than for standard equipment. All pipes in the machine were made from stainless, non-corrosive metal, which was not true of the standard equipment. The reserve tanks were glass-lined and the whole outfit was easily cleaned and sterilized.

The extract bottling equipment was not the first machinery built by Jewel employees. Throughout the Barrington plant were machines that were modified in some way or even built from the bottom up. The machinists at Jewel in their day-to-day operations found many parts which could be eliminated from standard equipment. Eliminating gadgets reduced Jewel operating and maintenance costs.

In 1938 - 1939, refining companies, breakfast food companies, and other firms had asked Jewel's permission to watch these machines in operation. The companies manufacturing such equipment for sale sent their own draftsmen and engineers to Barrington to see the operations ideas which six months before they called "unworkable".

Jewel received the All-American loving cup in the late 1930s when Jewel extract bottles were rated tops in an annual contest staged by American Packaging Magazine.

Lemon Extract

Golden — aromatic — pungent — palate stimulating. These are only a few of the thoughts that come to us when we see and use Jewel Lemon Extract. And the flavor — color — and odor— are there because only a pure lemon oil, lemon peel, certified grain alcohol are used in its manufacture. 2 oz. bottle. Price 41c. (P. S. C. 10c.)

From 1926, the above original advertisement and captions for Jewel Lemon Extract.

Quick Oats

"Steaming hot, and it only took three minutes! Jewel Quick Oats have been partially cooked by steam under pressure during the manufacturing process. They are wholesome and nutritious. May be used by all members of the family. Even the baby should have his oatmeal water made with them. They combine excellently with meats in patties, in cookies, muffins, and with fruits. Neat, attractive package, with instructions for using. 2 lb. 10 oz. package. Price 26c. (P. S. C. 5c.)

An original advertisement and captions, shown above, for Quick Oats.

In 1927 the above Jewel Toasted Thick Corn Flakes appeared in a Jewel News. Distributed by Jewel Tea Co., Inc., New York - Chicago.

The above Jewel Quick Oats were rich in Vitamin B1. Distributed by Jewel Tea Co., Inc., Barrington, Ill. The back listed directions for cooking and variations for using Jewel Quick Oats in recipes. *Author's Collection.*

Sold in Jewel Food Stores today, the above 1-lb. 2 oz. Jewel Corn Flakes was a vitamin fortified cereal. *Author's Collection.*

Shown above, one dozen Jewel selected Grade A large white eggs. *Hedges Collection.*

The above 3-lbs. Jewel rice was good for breakfast, lunch, or dinner. Note the exceptional example of the Jewel logo. *Nemluvil Collection.*

Waffle Mix

In April 1946, a brand new mix was available to Jewel customers, Jewel Waffle Mix. Since Jewel specialized in prepared mixes, it was only natural that they should add this American favorite to their rapidly expanding list of mixes available to Jewel customers.

It seems that Jewel's food chemists were experimenting with a formula for waffles and came up with a batch to be served to visitors in Jewel's employees' cafeteria in Barrington. The waffles received praises and the question was asked, "Why don't you make a waffle mix for Jewel customers?" At that time, the only reason "why not" was the shortage of certain ingredients. When they were made available, in small quantities, Jewel Waffle Mix was born. The mix was packaged in a new vermilion and gray box.

Rich Fragrant Jewel Coffee The Finest Coffee You Can Buy!

"That quality gave Jewel an advantage over so many other coffees. Jewel coffee experts chose from the world's fine coffees and carefully blended them to provide the same good cup of coffee every time. This special blending of choice coffee beans gave Jewel Coffee richer flavor and fuller body. Such distinctive goodness could always be expected because Jewel's process of flash-roasting insured an even roast of every coffee bean. You could be sure Jewel Coffee was rich and fresh, because it was rushed straight from the roaster to you — delivered fresh to your door!"

The delicious flavor and aroma you wanted in your cup of coffee could be found only in a coffee that was rich and fresh, much like those shown below.

Jewel coffees were purchased, processed, tested, packaged and delivered with the most exacting standards and under the most modern conditions. Only from Jewel could American home-makers buy coffees so delicious, pure, uniform and fresh.

JEWEL CUP

JEWEL CUP has been called the popular blend because it is so universally accepted as a quality coffee, at a remarkably reasonable price. Always uniform; always fresh and delightful. Ground. 2 and 3-lb. pkgs.

The lid shown above on the "Jewel Brand Coffee" is embossed with "Jewel Tea Co.". No "Inc." appeared after the Jewel Tea Co. logo which indicates a date before 1916. *Hamilton Collection.*

Your guests will always be pleased when you serve them Jewel coffee. What else could you buy to serve them that would be more satisfying?

Jewel coffees are perfectly roasted and each package is delivered quickly and carefully to you, assuring freshness and quality.

JEWEL BEST is a mild blend, wholly satisfying in flavor and aroma. Par excellence in coffee. This is the most popular Jewel blend today —try it! Ground or in the bean. 2 and 3-lb. pkgs.

Look for the best in flavor and aroma—you will find both in any of these fine blends.

The above advertisement and original captions for "Jewel Cup Coffee" was taken from The Jewel News 1926.

The Jewel Brand Coffee container, shown above, with paper label is approximately 9-1/4" tall and 5-1/2" in diameter and holds 3-lbs. whole coffee. Note the picture of the Washington Boulevard and Ada Street building. This coffee was priced at $1.10. *Hamilton Collection.*

Shown above, a different view of Jewel Brand Coffee. Again note the logo that appears on this exceptional container of coffee. *Hamilton Collection.*

Coffee was one of the prime sellers for Jewel Tea. Shown above, a 2-lb. "West Coast Blend Coffee" product that was roasted daily. It was a rich, full-bodied coffee. Roasted and packed by - Jewel Tea Co., Inc., Los Angeles, Cal. The lid of the coffee tin is embossed with the same Bell and Jewel Tea logo that appears on the particle paper label. A valuable coupon was enclosed in this package. During the mid-1960s the Los Angeles plant closed. *Lemons Collection.*

A portion of the paper label is missing from the above "West Coast Blend Coffee. Jewel Tea Co., Los Angeles, Ca". *Lemons Collection.*

The above 2-lb. Jewel Blend Coffee, dated circa 1948, advertised as the World's Finest Coffee and Roaster Fresh. Roasted and packed by Jewel Tea Co., Inc., Barrington, Ill. *Nemluvil Collection.*

The above 1-lb. Royal Jewel Coffee, "Famous For Freshness". Distributed by Jewel Food Stores - A Department of Jewel Tea Co., Inc., Chicago, Ill. *Nemluvil Collection.*

Shown above, a full 2-lb. carton of Jewel Blend Coffee, "Makes The Whole Meal Better". Roasted and packed by Jewel Tea Co., Inc., Barrington, Ill. - Anaheim, Cal. *Byerly Collection.*

The above 32 oz. (2 lb.) Jewel Blend Coffee, roasted and packaged by Jewel Companies, Inc., Barrington, Illinois 60010. Tested and approved by Mary Dunbar Jewel Homemaker Institute. *Hedges Collection.*

The exceptional one pound tin, shown above, held Jewel Brand Pan Fired Japan Tea. It was packed with special care by the Jewel Tea Co., Chicago, U.S.A. A paper label appears on this tin container. *Hamilton Collection.*

A clear view of this exceptional tin. On close examination of this tin, the Bar N' Circle logo can be seen on the very bottom on the trim section. The logo appears on every side, top, and bottom in which the trim strip is intact. *Hamilton Collection.*

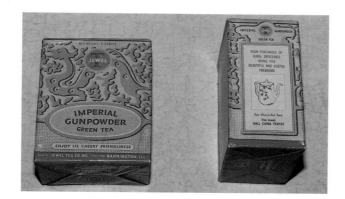

"Enjoy Its Cheery Friendliness" appears on the above "Imperial Gunpowder Green Tea", which shows the front and side section of a full sealed container of tea. *Busch Collection.*

The three tins at right display Jewel Tea: L-R, 24 bags of Orange, Spice, Naturally Flavored, New Weight 1.5 oz; 24 bags of Earl Grey, 1.5 oz; 24 bags of Strawberry, Naturally Flavored, Net Wt. 1.5 oz. *Weales Collection.*

Shown above, 4 oz. tin of Jewel extra fancy Darjeeling blend Tea. *Moos Collection.*

Shown above, Jewel 48 tea bags, finest blend orange pekoe and pekoe cut black tea. Net weight 3-3/4 oz. Note illustration of Autumn Leaf china on cover. *Hedges Collection.*

"Enjoy the cheery friendliness of refreshing iced tea throughout the entire year", appeared on the above carton of Jewel 24 Jumbo Iced Tea Bags. Net Weight is 6 oz. and 1 bag made 1 quart. Jewel Home Shopping Service. *Byerly Collection.*

48 bags of Orange Pekoe and Pekoe Jewel tea bags, shown above. Packed by Jewel Tea Co., Inc., Jewel Park, Barrington, Illinois circa 1950s. *Hedges Collection.*

The above was packed by Jewel Tea Co. Inc., Jewel Park, Barrington, Ill. Oolong and Gunpowder mixed tea. Enjoy its cheery friendliness. *Hedges Collection.*

The Tea Bags

In 1946, the tea bags that were delivered were something special! Made from a fine texture, tasteless, ordorless head sealing paper, these tea bags gave a clearer cup of tea. Customer's noticed the extra large size bag, that allowed more complete extraction of all the fine tea flavor. Jewel Tea experts were thinking of everything.

Those tea bags, in 1946, were the first to be packed in Jewel's Barrington plant, on a new postwar packaging machine. Jewel was proud of this new machine and wanted their customers to know what it meant to them in the way of better tea bags.

A writer for The Jewel News went down to see the new tea bag line and to see how the machine was worked and was operated. The writer proclaimed the machine did everything but drink the tea! He had seen a long strip of heat sealing paper fed into the machine from one side, the blended tea poured down a pipe from the floor above, and the paper and tea came together in the center. Little tea bags were then formed and pushed out a metal chute.

After watching the intricate mechanism closely, the writer could see how the paper was instantaneously heat-sealed, the edges crimped, and then each bag was cut apart from the one next to it.

Considered most miraculous was the fact that this machine placed the same amount of tea into each filter bag. The quantity was controlled by an adjustment in the angle of the pipe through which the tea flowed. This tea was the same high quality that anyone was getting in Jewel's previously produced Black Tea.

On the packaging of the tea bag carton appeared a picturesque dragon.

Green Tea

In late 1946, Jewel customers could begin buying Green Tea from their friendly Jewel Man. It was a delicious blend of fine, unfermented green teas, carefully treated to retain their rare, delicate tang and pleasing aroma.

New York Jewel buyers were successful in buying a large shipment of green tea. As soon as it had been processed and packed in the Barrington plant, the Jewel Man had it in his basket.

It had been a long time since customers last served this delicate tea. The war had seriously curtailed its production, and it would be years before the supply was to reach pre-war levels.

Jewel customers were the first to serve Green Tea again because Jewel was among the first to have it.

Jewel noted the difference between Green and Black Teas. Green Tea was treated immediately after the leaves were picked so that the pores of the leaves were sealed and the green tea was preserved in it's natural green state. For Black Tea, the leaves were exposed to the air for a length of time while nature worked a distinct change in the nature of the leaves so that they were entirely changed.

This difference in leaf treatment accounted for the difference in taste. Jewel indicated that tea was mankind's most popular beverage. Three times as many people in the world were drinking tea were drinking coffee. This is a considerable number as in 1946 there were five hundred million coffee drinkers in the world!

The above carton contained 48 bags of Jewel Tea. *Hedges Collection.*

Tea

For cool, refreshing iced tea, there is the rich, amber colored Jewel Orange Pekoe Tea with its flavor of unsurpassed deliciousness. Orange Pekoe (black tea) Price $1.00 per pound or $.50 per half pound (P.S.C. 10c and 5c respectively).

The above original Jewel Orange Pekoe and Pekoe, advertisement and captions appeared in a 1926 Jewel News.

The above two tins each have a different logo. Top tin held Jewel Tea Co., Breakfast Cocoa. Bottom tin is believed to have held either coffee or tea. Note early Jewel logo. *Hedges Collection.*

It is believed the tin, shown above, may have held tea. The tin is in excellent condition, even though part of the paper label is missing. The tin is 3" high, 4-1/2" across and 14" in circumference. The paper label reads; "TRADE THE JEWEL MARK", The word TRADE is above THE and MARK is below THE. *Hamilton Collection.*

Shown above, the round lid to the above tin. Printed on this lid is, "REGISTERED JUNE 6, 1876 U.S. PATENT OFFICE". *Hamilton Collection.*

The first appearance of a Victory Package is in the Jewel News 1942. Numerous products of that era (World War II) carry this "Victory Package" symbol.

Circa 1930s, it was a rich flavored "Jewel Cocoa", shown above. The 5" tall container held 1 lb. and on the back gave cocoa frosting and cocoa recipes. It was a wonderful red-brown cocoa, so rich in cocoa butter as to give genuine chocolate flavor to cornstarch puddings, bread puddings, pies, cakes, icings and, of course, the nourishing cup of hot chocolate. In 1931 it sold for 35¢. *Nemluvil Collection.*

It was quick, smooth, creamy and rich. The above Jewel chocolate flavored Milk Shake Mix. *Byerly Collection.*

The above 1942 - 1945 unique Jewel Tea, 1 pound can of Chocolate Rich! Cocoa. Packed by Jewel Tea Co., Inc., Jewel Park, Barrington, ILL. Note "Victory Package" symbol in upper corner. This is not a paper container. *Pero Collection.*

The above pure Cocoa was "Healthful and Nourishing" for the whole family. It was also "Tested and Approved by Mary Dunbar", Net Weight was 1-lb. Jewel Tea Co., Inc., Jewel Park, Barrington, Ill. *Byerly Collection.*

The above One Pound Cocoa was "Rich In Flavor". Jewel Tea Co., Inc., New York - Chicago. *Byerly Collection.*

The above pure Cocoa was "Healthful and Nourishing" for the whole family. It was also "Tested and Approved by Mary Dunbar", Net Weight was 1-lb. Jewel Tea Co., Inc., Jewel Park, Barrington, Ill. *Byerly Collection.*

The above Jewel Tea 1-lb. container of Chocolate Flavored Malted Milk Mixture was "A Rich Creamy Tempting Drink". It contained "viobin" a Vitamin B food concentrate. Jewel Tea Co., Inc., Jewel Park, Barrington, Ill. *Byerly Collection.*

The above Jewel Tea Cocoa, circa 1917 - 1918, packed by Jewel Tea Co., Inc., Chicago, Ill. Note scale logo on front. *Byerly Collection.*

Jewel's Instant Cocoa Mix, manufactured by Jewel Tea Co., Inc., Barrington, Illinois. *Byerly Collection.*

Jewel chocolate flavored desert mix, shown above. Jewel Tea Co. Inc., Jewel Park, Barrington, Ill. *Byerly Collection.*

Jewel's Jumbo 125 - 12" straws fit King size 16 oz. bottles. Prefect for any drink. Children of all ages liked them. *Byerly Collection.*

Cleaners, Soaps and Beauty Products

Soap Powder

Heavy, dirty work can be done with Jewel Soap Powder. It has no ingredient harmful to fabric or hands. Dissolves easily, forming a heavy suds.

Shown above, a original "Jewel Soap Powder" advertisement and caption that appeared in a 1926 Jewel News.

Chip Soap

Jewel Chip Soap is fine, neutral laundry soap in thin, easily and quickly dissolved chips. It lightens your work because it lessens your labor. It is economical to use, for there is no waste. Jewel Chip Soap is an excellent cleanser. It may be used for every purpose for which soap is required in your daily household uses. 20 ounce package $.25— P. S. C. $.05.

The above original "Jewel Chip Soap" advertisement and caption appeared in a 1926 Jewel News.

Velvetouch

Cool your skin with this fine skin jelly made with a glycerin base. It is delicately perfumed with a combination of five perfumes, of which Jasmine is outstanding. Use after shaving, dish washing, manicuring, or before powdering. Because of its base it will not grow hair. Price, Jar 25c (P. S. C. 5c).

The original advertisement and captions for Velvetouch Dusting Powder, shown above, appeared in a 1926 Jewel News.

A Great Little Labor-Saver

Make water soft and save on soap. Any soap will quickly make suds in water to which Jewel Powdered Ammonia has been added. It "breaks" the water. It also cleanses, and how it does brighten w i n d o w s when added to cleaning water! Dissolves easily. A household treat. Cardboard carton, with metal top and base. Two 12-ounce cans. Price 25c. (P. S. C. 5c.)

The above great little labor saver appeared in a 1927 Jewel News, "Jewel Powdered Ammonia Compound".

Jewel Cleanser Cleans, Scours, Renews

A powder which will scour but not s c r a t c h. Jewel Cleanser is a fine white powder, grit free, and non-abrasive. Shake it freely on enamel ware, especially on bathroom fixtures, and it will renew the smooth, white finish. Highly recommended for cleaning enamel and tin pots and pans, and so easy to apply. Does not hurt the hands. Three 1-pound cans per sale. Price 28c. (P. S. C. 5c.)

The above Jewel Cleanser that "Cleans, Scours, Renews" appeared in a 1927 Jewel News.

JEWEL LAUNDRY TABLETS will serve you well. They loosen dirt, help to remove stains. whitening clothes and softening water. 20 tablets. Regular price................. **25c**

(Profit Sharing Credit 5c)

The above original "Jewel Laundry Tablets" advertisement appeared in a 1930 Jewel News.

In 1934, Jewel conducted a contest open to Jewel customers to name a new soap product. The idea behind the winning name was — it softens water — to make soap go further. The grand prize was a complete set of Club Aluminum Hammered Crafts-man Cookware or one of 30 other prizes. The contest ended May 30, 1934. In Issue No. 9 of the Jewel News, the grand prize winner was announced as being D.S. Browning of Iron Mountain, Michigan and a list of runners-up was printed. The winning name was announced in Issue No. 10, in 1934 as "U-NO-ME".

In 1938, Jewel advertised this product for hard water. With a little "U-No-Me", the amount of soap needed for rich suds was reduced. It claimed to save on soap when used in the washing of greasy dishes and extra-dirty play clothes. 2-1/2-lb. package, 5¢ premium credit.

Shown above 2-lb. 8-oz., Grano Granulated Soap Concentrated Cleaning Power! Made in California - Distributed by Jewel Tea Co, Inc., Los Angeles, California. *Lemons Collection.*

Shown at left Grano Granulated Soap, 2-lbs. 8-oz. Distributed by Jewel Tea Co., Inc., Jewel Park, Barrington, Ill. *Byerly Collection.*

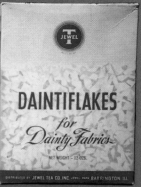

Shown above, two different packaging for Jewel Daintiflakes. *Hedges Collection.*

Distributed by Jewel Tea Co. Barrington, Illinois, the above 5 refreshing Pine Scented Bars of Jewel Pine Soap, circa 1957. *Nemluvil Collection.*

Shown above, Jewel Pine Toilet Soap. *Byerly Collection.*

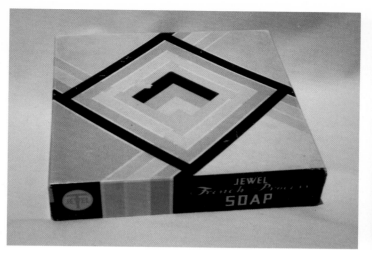

The words "Jewel French Process Soap" appear on the circa 1931 carton shown above. Six pastel colored soap bars are stamped with "Jewel French Process" on one side and Jewel "T" on the other. The carton is a 7" square x 1-1/4". Circa 1931. *Lemons Collection.*

The popularity of Jewel French Process Soap, shown above, spoke for itself in 1938. It lathered freely in hand or in soft water and was a bigger, longer lasting cake of soap. Distributed by Jewel Tea Co., Inc., Barrington, Illinois. *Byerly Collection.*

Shown above, two different packagings for the French Process Soap. The cartons held the same soap, the only difference was in the packaging. *Hedges Collection.*

The above 4-1/2" high x 3" diameter cleanser can held 14-oz. of Glorex Cleanser Lemon Scented. "Wipes Away Grease and Stain — Never Scratches!" Distributed by Jewel Tea Co., Jewel Park, Barrington, Ill. *Lemons Collection.*

"Sudsing Glorex Cleanser" appears on the back side of the above Glorex Cleanser. *Lemons Collection.*

Circa 1930s Jewel Talcum Powder, shown above, held 13-oz. Distributed by Jewel Tea Co. Inc., Jewel Park, Barrington, Ill. *Nemluvil Collection.*

Jewel's Chatnay Talcum can, shown above. *Byerly Collection.*

3-oz. Sara Lotion and two cakes of lilac supreme bath soap, shown above.
Distributed by Jewel Tea Co., Inc., Barrington, Ill. *Hedges Collection.*

The original, unopened Velvetouch Dusting Powder, shown above. This
container held 5-oz. and was distributed by Jewel Tea Co., Inc.,
Barrington, Ill. *Byerly Collection.*

Shown above, 9-oz. Jewel Medicated Skin Cream. *Hedges Collection.*

Circa 1957, the above 11-oz. Jetco moth proofing spray. Manufactured by Jewel Tea Co., Inc., Barrington, Ill. *Nemluvil Collection.*

The above carton of Jewel scouring pads contain three original scouring pads. *Author's Collection.*

Jewel automatic bowl clean, 6 oz., shown above. *Hedges Collection.*

Shown above, Jetco new laundry no rub. Jewel Home Shopping Service. *Hedges Collection.*

13 oz. of Jewel Spray Pre-wash Spotter, shown above. *Schwartz Collection.*

32 oz. each HD Concentrated Fabric Softener with the light touch. Jewel Companies Inc., Barrington, Illinois 60010. *Schwartz Collection.*

Two different containers of Jewel Clean 'N Shine. Each container held 32 Fl. ozs. *Schwartz Collection.*

1950s - 1960s, 32 Fl. oz., Jetco Laundry Brightener shown on the left. *Schwartz Collection.*

2 qts. of Jetco fluff, shown above. *Schwartz Collection.*

Shown above, Jewel hand cleaner lotion. This is a paper label. Distributed by Jewel Home Shopping Service, Barrington, Illinois. *Schwartz Collection.*

Shown above, 12 oz. of Jewel no-dust. *Schwartz Collection.*

An original advertisement with captions, shown at right, for Jewel Toilet Soaps from 1926.

Toilet Soaps

Every toilet soap should have a pure base, properly neutralized and capable of producing an abundant lather. The question of color and odor then becomes a matter of personal preference.

Jewel Toilet Soaps please the majority. They are all pure, high grade, carefully made toilet necessities. You will find *your* favorite among them.

Pure Jewel,   Price 30c for 3 cakes (P. S. C. 5c)
Hardwater,   Price 30c for 3 cakes (P. S. C. 5c)
Baby Castile, Price 30c for 3 cakes (P. S. C. 5c)

White Floating Soap

Jewel White Floating is a superior utility soap, for use in toilet, bath or dainty housework and laundry. 5 cakes 40c (P. S. C. 5c).

Present day (2 qt.) Jewel Food Store Heavy Duty Laundry Detergent®, shown above. *Author's Collection.*

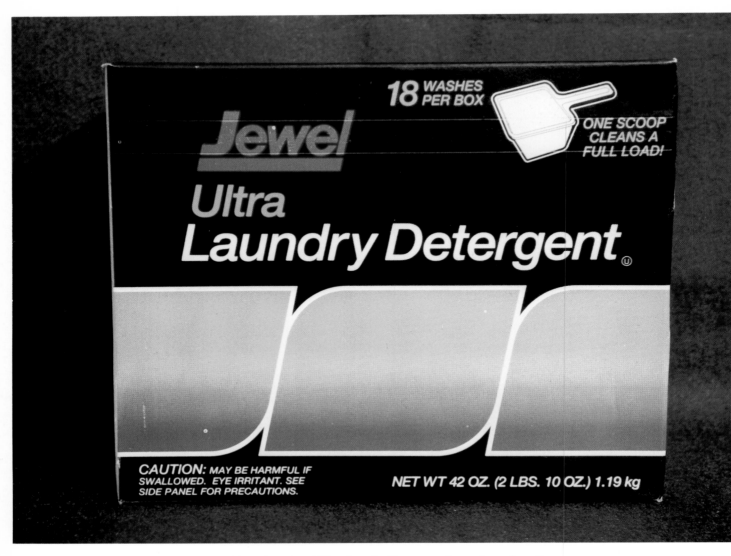

The 2 lbs. 10 oz. Jewel Ultra Laundry Detergent, shown above, is available in Jewel Food Stores today. *Author's Collection.*

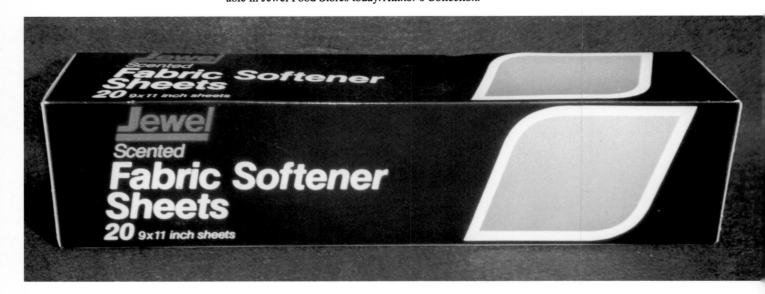

Shown above, 20 - 9 x 11" Jewel scented fabric softener sheets available in Jewel Food Stores today. *Author's Collection.*

Shown above, a carton of 20 Jewel trash can liners. These liners fit 20 - 30 gallon trash cans. *Author's Collection.*

The young fellow's mother, shown right, has just heard the best news. A completely new Jewel Dental Cream would soon be offered to Jewel customers. After almost three years' of experimentation in a laboratory and in many homes, Jewel had a dental cream justifying all enthusiasm in 1938.

The flavor was unique and could not be duplicated in any tooth paste purchased at any local drugstore. "The mint flavor leaves the mouth delightfully fresh and clean." It had an individual tone and taste of its own.

The ingredients were pure and scientifically balanced. Offered in a giant-size tube and at a low price, Jewel believed it was the best buy on the market.

The "Dusting Paper" at right was used for cleaning, dusting and polishing. It was Convenient - Sanitary - Labor Saving. Measures 11-3/4" long x 2-1/4" across, and was 50 feet in length. Note Jewel logo partially visible in center of package. *Lemons Collection.*

Shown above is a different view of the "Dusting Paper". This paper dates from circa 1942, and was distributed by Jewel Tea Co., Inc., Jewel Park, Barrington, Ill. *Nemluvil Collection.*

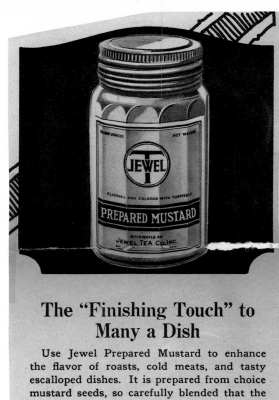

The "Finishing Touch" to Many a Dish

Use Jewel Prepared Mustard to enhance the flavor of roasts, cold meats, and tasty escalloped dishes. It is prepared from choice mustard seeds, so carefully blended that the "aftertaste" is most pleasing. It comes to you ready for instant use. Handy when preparing sauces and dressings. 12-ounce jar, price 25c. (P.S.C. 5c.)

The same packaging for Jewel Peanut Butter also held Jewel Prepared Mustard, shown above, in 1927.

"Um-m-m, It's Good," and So Convenient!

Jewel Peanut Butter, made from fine, selected, freshly roasted peanuts, with absolutely nothing added but salt, is ready to use when it reaches you. Because of its tasty flavor it can be used as the base of many dishes: soups, cakes, cookies, candies, sandwiches, and salads; and, for school lunches, with Jewel Crackers. 12-ounce jar, price 35c. (P.S.C. 5c.)

The above original advertisement and captions for Jewel Peanut Butter appeared in a Jewel News in 1927.

Honey Flavored

What a treat are these honey-flavored, crisp, graham crackers, with a glass of milk, for midday lunch! Or, they can be made into any number of good dishes; nutritious puddings, desserts, fancy tea wafers, sandwiches, and at this time of the year, the Graham Cracker Strawberry Short Cake, made with alternating layers of crackers, whipped cream, and strawberries is just delicious! Always fresh and sweet. 22-ounce package, price 35c. (P.S.C. 5c.)

The advertisement at right and captions for Jewel Graham Crackers appeared in a 1927 Jewel News.

Distributed by Jewel Tea Co., Inc., Jewel Part, Barrington, Ill., the one pound carton of Jewel Graham Crackers at right was fresh–crunchy–delicious–crisp. *Hedges Collection.*

Just add milk and whip, you had the perfect whip dessert topping. The carton shown below held a twin pack and made one quart of whipped topping. *Blow Collection.*

Shown above, Jewel Whipping Cream mix, packaged by Jewel Tea Co., Inc., Jewel Park, Barrington, Ill. *Hedges Collection.*

In November 1929, Jewel offered a 2-lb. jar of Holiday candy for the home or to be used as a gift. The Mary Dunbar candy jar held an additional 1-lb. (3-lbs total) than the offer of 1929 and made an attractive gift, one that all could enjoy. Approximately 12" high with a metal screw on lid, the candy had 100% filled centers and sold for 95¢ in 1929.

A blue and gold paper label appears on the front of the jar at right and reads: "Mary Dunbar Candy - Soft Centers - 3-lbs. Net Weight. Distributed by Jewel Tea Co., Inc., New York - Chicago.

The jar was produced by Anchor Hocking and carries the "HA" marking on the bottom with a series of numbers. *Author's Collection.*

1950s - 1960s, 3-1/2 oz. of Jewel imitation butterscotch flavor pudding and pie filling, shown above. *Blow Collection.*

Shown above, three cartons of Jewel Jell, in orange, lemon and lime flavors. Jewel Tea Co., Inc., Jewel Park, Barrington, Ill. *Schwartz Collection.*

Jewel Jell natural raspberry flavor, shown above. Manufactured by Jewel Tea Co., Inc., Jewel Park, Barrington, Ill. *Byerly Collection.*

The above Jewel Jell, a "Gelatin Dessert", was offered in net weight of 4 ounce jars. Pure lemon flavor, imitation strawberry flavor and imitation cherry flavor. Other flavors may have been available. Manufactured by Jewel Tea Co., Inc., Jewel Park, Barrington, Ill. *Byerly Collection.*

Jewel Macaroni, Spaghetti, Noodles

An original promotional photograph, shown below, for Jewel Elbow Macaroni, Spaghetti and Egg Noodles from the late 1930s. Kentucky Macaroni Co., of Louisville, Kentucky produced Jewel Macaroni Products.

Jewel 16 oz. Mayonnaise and 14 oz. Peanut Butter are promoted in the historical photograph above. Accompanied with an Autumn Leaf plate, "Radiance" Custard, and Ivanhoe flatware complete the picture. Any child would have enjoyed an after school treat like Jewel promoted. *Barrington Archives.*

Jewel Lime Flavored Jell and Jewel Mayonnaise set the scene in the above historic promotional photograph. It is believed the china is referred to as "Floral Dresden". Jewel Jell was offered in six flavors. *Barrington Archives.*

Jewel Jell in Lime, Cherry and Strawberry would have attracted the attention of any child when the historical photograph on the left promoted this product. Accompanied by fresh fruit served in a Autumn Leaf salad bowl, Jewel Jell was served on a bed of lettuce on a Autumn Leaf plate with a cup of fresh coffee served in a regular dinnerware style cup and saucer and a "Madrid" glass of fresh water. The flatware again is "Ivanhoe". *Barrington Archives.*

Promotioning Jewel Handicut Waxed Paper, manufactured by the Automtic Paper Mach. Co. Inc., Elizabeth, N.J. The carton contained 80 ft by 12" wide waxed paper. The rolled sandwich or pastry appears on a "Madrid" plate. *Barrington Archives.*

Jewel products were tested in Jewel laboratories by highly skilled chemist as shown in the photograph above. The only information on the back says "Chemist in Chicago Laboratory, early 1920s". Note the Jewel Gloss Starch near the microscope and other Jewel products in the far right hand corner. *Barrington Archives.*

Above is a highly detailed photograph with a variety of Jewel products being tested by a chemist in a Chicago laboratory in the early 1920s. Note the various Jewel soap products and the variety of Jewel spices: Cinnamon, Allspice, Mustard, Black Pepper and Nutmeg. *Barrington Archives.*

Grano laundry soap is being tested in the later photograph shown above. The Chief Chemist J.M. Shapira oversees the operation of the Jewel laboratory. *Barrington Archives.*

Above Chief Chemist J.M. Shapira analyzing Jewel Malted Milk Mixture. The chart behind the Malted Milk is a Vitamin Chart and the diagram is of a Wheat Kernel. *Barrington Archives.*

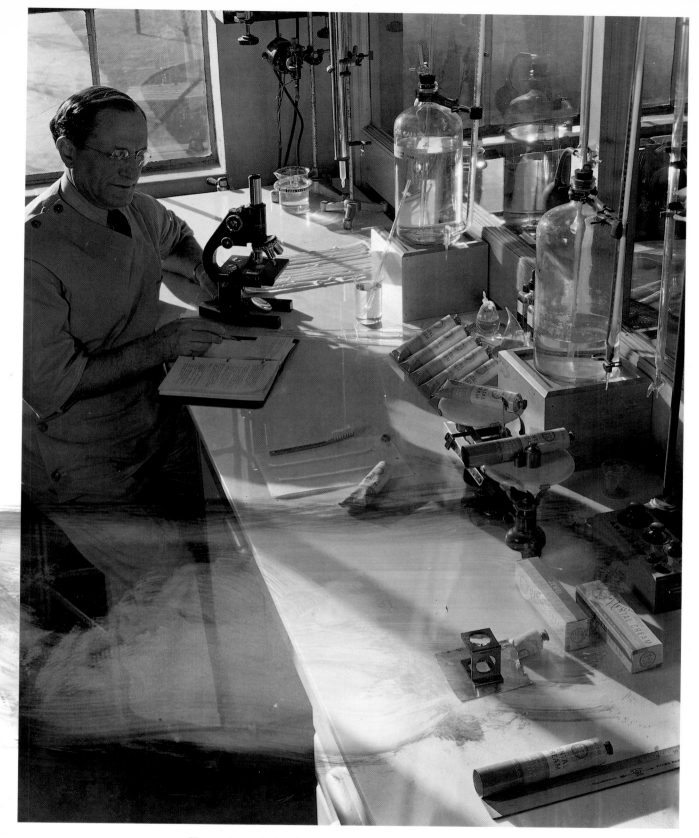

Shown above, in Jewel Laboratory, Jewel Dental Cream is being analyzed by Chief Chemist J.M. Shapira. *Barrington Archives.*

Two unknown Jewel employees package Jewel Jell in the historical photograph above. The young man to the right holds flat packaging cartons that he feeds into the stacked supply in front of him. The young lady is believed to be operating the machinery. Note the process from flat packaging to the filled carton in the center of the photograph. Look closely at the young lady's freshly starched uniform and cap with the Jewel logo. *Barrington Archives.*

In the early 1950s, even the above postman worked hand in hand with your friendly Jewel Man.

Working together they made a great team! They made it better, faster and were a more convenient Jewel Home Service team. With the Postman, the friendly Jewel Man furnished the customer with a greater selection of merchandise, a greater range of style, of color choice, and size.

Whether your Jewel Man or your Postman delivered your purchase, Jewel paid the delivery charges.

As I was packing the manuscript and photographs to mail to the publisher, I received the photographs of the colorful "MARY DUNBAR Coffee" can shown above and on the right. This pound of regular grind coffee was "Distributed by Jewel Food Stores Chicago, a Department of Jewel Tea Co., Inc., Barrington, Ill". This key type opener tin has the number 2263 imprinted in the top, see photograph below. This may indicated the year "1963". Jewel was into using the "DUNBAR" name during that era. *Hamilton Collection.*

64

CHAPTER 2
AUTUMN LEAF KITCHENWARE
AND DINNERWARE

One of the most important decisions The Hall China Company of East Liverpool, Ohio ever made was that of entering into an agreement with The Jewel Tea Company to make the Autumn Leaf pattern china. That became an exclusive Jewel pattern, designed by Hall.

Jewel's connection with Hall China dates back to the mid 1920s. Hall teapots were premiums during the 1920s and in the early 1940s the Morning Glory pattern was carried by Jewel, during the 1950s Hall's Cameo Rose dinnerware graced many Sunday tables.

Of all the Jewel premiums, the Autumn Leaf pattern remains the highest in demand today. Collectors nationwide search those pieces out. Unusual, often referred to as rare or one-of-a-kind, pieces demand astronomical prices.

Condition Factor

Autumn Leaf China that is cracked, broken, stained, or mended bring a very small percentage in the secondary market. The majority of collectors will pass those pieces by. Those in mint condition demand high dollars.

Collectors search for pieces in perfect condition. Gold on any select piece must be brilliant and complete and have a polished shine. Coloring should include a deep, creamy background with the decal rich in shades of brown and orange detail that form the stylized floral pattern. The gold line on the edge of each piece enhances the rich simplicity of the pattern. The surface is highly glazed for extra smoothness.

Top and bottoms of most pieces could be easily replaced at the time if damaged, as they could be purchased separately.

Tangible proof of tireless service is noted when pieces have nicks, chips, tatters and tears. Only those pieces of sentimental value that show tireless service are retained by collectors. There's a story that goes along with every purchase, whether its damaged or in mint condition.

The China was said to be so rich and elegant, yet so sturdy, that homemakers all over the United States marveled at the way it stood up under everyday use. That's the reason Hall "Autumn" Dinnerware remained the favorite of Jewel customers for years. It had all the grace, charm and beauty of the most expensive dinnerware. Yet it was priced within reach of the most budget-minded homemaker.

American semi-vitreous dinnerware is made of approximately the same mixture of minerals as china, but it has been treated a little differently. Semi-vitreous dinnerware is molded somewhat thicker than china and fired at not quite such high temperatures. Because of this it is very durable and will stand a great deal of wear and use. The deep glaze completely seals the somewhat porous center of each piece.

Hall China Jewel Tea Autumn Leaf was "Tested and Approved by Mary Dunbar — Jewel Homemakers Institute" and carried the famous backstamps shown on the right.

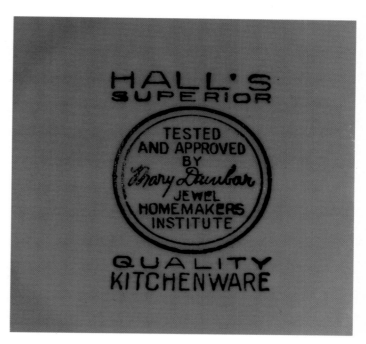

Made by the Hall China Company, East Liverpool, Ohio, the above Jewel Tea 3-1/2 qt. mixing bowl with the Autumn Leaf decal was first introduced in 1933. Note the paper label. *Preo Collection.*

Shown above, a closer view of the paper label that reads: HALL Superior Quality KITCHENWARE Guaranteed Against Breakage In Oven Heat And Refrigerator Cold. *Preo Collection.*

Two smaller size bowls, the 2 qt. and the small 1 qt. bowls, were added by Christmas that year to complete the three-piece set. These Autumn Leaf pieces remained in line until they were discontinued in 1976. *Author's Collection.*

The above utility/mixing bowl set is a nest of bowls of graduated sizes made to fit inside each other. This set became one of Jewel's most successful offerings and has started many collections. *Author's Collection.*

The nested utility bowls fit perfectly into the metal cake safe, as shown at right. The cake safe provided a covering for the bowls or could be used to carry a covered dish to a family function. *Byerly Collection.*

The above 9-1/2" round cake plate is one of the most common found pieces. Introduced in 1937 and discontinued in 1976, the cake plate was multi-purposed. *Author's Collection.*

The 9-1/2" round cake plate backstamp is shown above. *Author's Collection.*

The round cake plate fit perfectly in the metal cake safe for easy handling, as shown above. *Author's Collection.*

The 9-1/2" round cake plate was promoted periodically as a hot pad liner and could be used under the Hall Autumn Leaf Coffee Server as an underplate, as shown above. *Author's Collection.*

Introduced in the late 1950s, the above 3-1/2" high, 9-1/2" diameter cake plate with metal base, had a slightly beveled edge to keep cakes from sliding. The base was tarnish-resistant and doubled as a candleholder. *Author's Collection.*

The cake plate above showing the reversed side, with backstamp and metal base. *Author's Collection.*

Introduced at the same time was the all purpose candy dish server, shown on the right. 4-3/4" high, 6" diameter, the base was also tarnish-resistant and doubled as a candleholder. In 1960 both pieces sold for $4.95 each. *Byerly Collection.*

The tarnish-resistant candleholders, shown above, that also served as bases to the above cake plate and candy dish. *Byerly Collection.*

In 1935, for Jewel's 36th anniversary, the company introduced a special premium, the above 1-1/2 quarts or 6 cups capacity covered casserole. *Author's Collection.*

The double-duty lid, shown at right, could be used as a baking dish, pie pan or serving platter. *Author's Collection.*

The custard cup on the right was attractive, sturdy and did not tip easily. They were part of a sextet of 6 ounce "Radiance" individual custard cups shaped like the nested 3 piece mixing bowls and were introduced in 1936. One of the most plentiful items found in today's market. The individual cups hold a serving for one, and could be used for desserts, puddings, jello and custards. *Author's Collection.*

The 1936 "Rayed" cookie jar shown below was introduced by Jewel Tea in time to arrive in homes by Christmas. Selling for $1.50, this cookie jar was only offered until 1939. Many collectors refer to this jar as "Tootsie", as the handles and the top finial resemble a tootsie roll. The jar also could be used as a bean pot. *Author's Collection.*

The 1936 Cookie Jar shown for variation of right and left decals. Many collectors seek both variations. No logical interpretation can be given for these variations. *Jewel Payton Antiques.*

It wasn't until 1957 that Jewel Tea offered their second cookie jar, shown below, 7-1/2" high with two big ear-like handles that were easy to grip. The jar was designed by Eva Zeisel. Collectors often refer to this as the "Zeisel" jar. It was discontinued in 1969. *Author's Collection.*

Collectors of cookie jars are quick to point out a way to protect the lid and the base where they join. This may be accomplished by placing coffee filters under the lid, as shown at left. It isn't pretty but it does allow a cushion for the lid to rest on. *Author's Collection.*

In 1938, the 5-1/2 pint capacity "Ice-lipped Beverage" above was introduced. Designed with a handle for easy pouring and a shielded lip that held ice cubes inside the pitcher. *Author's Collection.*

The above black and white promotional photograph was used in a Jewel advertisement booklet, "Refreshing Iced Coffee and Tea", published by JEWEL TEA CO. Inc., Jewel Park, Barrington, Ill., during the late 1930s. The finished, published photograph showed only the "Ice-lipped Beverage", "Frosted Glasses" and a portion of the cream and sugar. *Barrington Archives.*

It had been brought to my attention that in a 1940 Jewel brochure promoting Jewel Iced Coffee there appears an Autumn Leaf Beverage pitcher without an ice lip.

After touring the Barrington headquarters and searching the archives, the original photograph was found. Upon examination of this photograph the pitcher does indeed have an ice lip. The original photograph appears above.

Open Stock

In May 1938, "Hall China" offered for sale "Open Stock" (mechandise, like china, available in sets, with individual pieces kept in stock for replacements or additions). The 13" platter No. 307-L, $1.00; 11" platter No. 307-K, 65¢; bread and butter plate No. 307-C, 25¢; pie plate No. 307-S, 35¢; cereal dish No. 307-G, 30¢; coupe soup or large flat soup No. 307-F, 40¢; and a salad plate.

Later the platters were advertised as 11-1/2" and 13-1/2", 6" bread and butter plate and the 7-3/4" salad plate. All were dropped in 1976. Only the oval 13-1/2" was reissued in 1978.

In 1940 the gravy boat, shown above, was introduced by Jewel Tea. *Author's Collection.*

In 1942 the 9" oval platter above was introduced which could be used as an underplate for the gravy boat, a pickle dish, relish dish or a small 9" cold meat platter. *Author's Collection.*

Both piece would be discontinued in 1976.

The above Marmalade was introduced in September 1938 measuring 3-1/2" in diameter. It rested on an underplate of 6". The lid opening allows for a spoon to be placed inside. In 1938, Vol. 16 No. 7 of the Jewel News promoted it as an attractive Marmalade. "A container worthy of serving your most prized preserves. Also nice for serving mayonnoise." The Marmalade was listed as Item No. 318 and sold for $1.25. A photograph appeared in the advertisement. *Author's Collection.*

The above Mustard jar measures 2-3/4" in diameter and the underplate 4-3/4". The mustard lid opening also allows for a spoon. In 1938, Vol. 16 No. 6 of the Jewel News this Mustard was promoted in an "Anniversary Sale - Special Anniversary - Gifts for the Bride. This attractive condiment jar in the Hall design may be used with any dishes. Just right for mustard, horseradish, sauces, etc. It's new, modern and extremely useful." Listed as Item No. 317 and sold for $1.00. A photograph of the Mustard Jar appeared in the advertisement. *Author's Collection.*

Hall China made no spoons for these jars. Both pieces were short-lived and are not listed after 1938.

The 9" Autumn Leaf plate, shown below, was introduced in 1936 and remained available until 1976. This plate was part of the initial offering. *Byerly Collection.*

Jewel introduced the 10" plate, 8" plate, 7-1/4" and a 6" plate in 1938 and continued to produce them until 1976, shown below. The 10" plates are one of the most sought after in the plate line. *Author's Collection.*

The 7-1/4" and the 6" plates are shown above. *Byerly Collection.*

In 1938, two oval platters where added to the dinnerware line: the 11-1/2" shown above, and the 13-1/2" shown below.

The above 5-1/2" fruit dish was introduced in 1936. The 6" cereal were
introduced in 1938. *Author's Collection.*

The above 9" round vegetable dish was introduced in 1937 and produced until 1939. Made for a short time, it is one of those difficult to find and expense pieces. *Byerly Collection.*

Offered from 1957 until 1976, the right oval divided vegetable bowl could serve two vegetables in the same bowl. The divided is harder to find than the undivided bowl and highly sought after by collectors of this famous china. *Author's Collection.*

Easy to find is the above oval undivided vegetable bowl introduced in 1939. It was re-issued in 1978. *Author's Collection.*

The above oval covered vegetable dish was introduced in 1940 and discontinued in 1976. *Author's Collection.*

Shown above, one of the most common and easily found Autumn Leaf bowls is the two-quart salad bowl. Introduced in 1937 and produced until 1976, it could be used for mixing and serving salads at the table, for fresh fruit, or as a flower bowl. *Author's Collection.*

The above 2-1/2 pint utility pitcher was introduced in 1937. It was perfect for pouring batter, whipping cream, eggs or any liquids. It was a handy size for table use. The heavy Hall ware also retained the original temperature of liquid. In January 1950 the utility pitcher was selling for 75¢, the same price as in 1940. *Author's Collection.*

Coupe soup bowl is a special pottery bowl approximately 7" to 8" inches in diameter that has no handles and is used to serve soup. The above 8-1/2" flat round soup was introduced in 1938 and produced until 1976. Two years later Hall China would re-issue this soup. *Author's Collection.*

Introduced in 1936, the above range set included the salt and pepper shakers and a covered drip. The salt and pepper shakers come in many configurations — left-handed, right-handed, etc.

In 1949 the three-piece range set was listed as being useful in the kitchen, decorative on the table, and the handles are easy to grasp when wet. Salt and pepper shaker are 4-1/2" high; dripping bowl holds 16 ounces. Listed as item number 5H105, the set sold for $2.25. *Author's Collection.*

The 2-3/8" ruffled base salt and pepper shakers, shown above, are often referred to as "Casper" where offerred in 1939.

In a Jewel Premium of 1940, the above were advertised as "Streamlined, modern, attractive salt and pepper shakers. Good capacity, but not too large." In sets of four, shown above, these shakers sold for only $1.50. Listed as Item No. 321. In 1961 they sold for 85 ¢ a piece. Note variation of motif — remember "Quality Control" was not of importance. *Author's Collection.*

In 1925, Jewel offered No. 760 — a fire proof porcelain baking dish. This was a beautiful piece of oven ware. White, delicately fluted and absolutely fireproof. It was an ideal dish for baking Jewel macaroni, spaghetti or noodles. Made by the Hall China Company, East Liverpool, Ohio. Priced at $1.25: Profit Sharing Credits (P.S.C.) or Cash. It is believed this piece was the second Hall piece offered by Jewel and would later become the 3-pint Autumn Leaf Motif Souffle/Casserole (French Baker). No photograph is available of No. 760.

Shown above, the 3-pint capacity Autumn Leaf Souffle/Casserole (French Baker) was introduced in 1935 and produced until 1976. This piece is quite common and can be found without much difficulty. *Author's Collection.*

The 2-pint Souffle/Casserole (French Baker), shown above, was introduced in 1966. The dish insured you of beautiful high souffles because of the straight sides on the inside. Item Number 5H 119 it was a 2-pint capacity and sold for $1.49. The 2-pint is one of the most sought after of the Autumn Leaf souffle pieces and, when located, can be quite expensive. *Byerly Collection.*

Introduced in 1966, the above individual Souffle/Casserole (French Baker) is commonly found. This individual baker is 4" in diameter, holds 10-ozs., and has many uses.

You may have difficulty finding the #499 individual Souffle/Casserole (French Baker) shown above. This appears larger than actual size. *Author's Collection.*

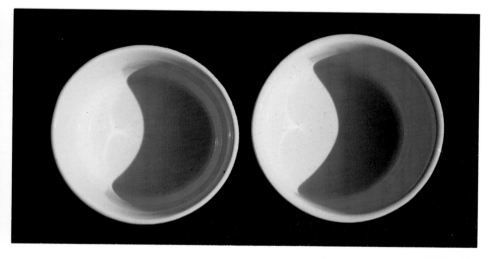

The baker on the right holds 10-ozs and measures 4-1/4" in diameter. This is approximately 1/4" larger than the original baker on the left. The #499 baker is not a 1978 re-issued piece, note the backstamp in the photograph shown below. *Author's Collection.*

Manufactured from 1966 - 1976, the above 12 oz. individual oval Ft. Pitt baker. You could bake and serve in the same dish. *Author's Collection.*

The inside of the 12 ounce individual oval Ft. Pitt baker shown above. This piece can be somewhat difficult to find and the price is constantly rising.

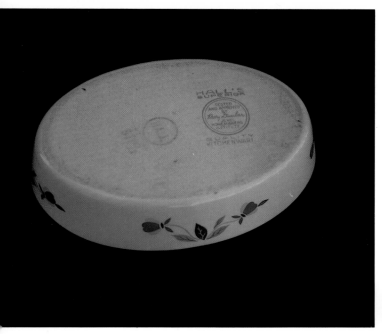

Shown above, the double backstamp on the 12 ounce Ft. Pitt baker. *Author's Collection.*

There are two known rare 10" Autumn Leaf oval "Fort Pitt" Bakers. Each holds 2-pints. I was unable to locate the owners and have been unable to locate any documentation of these piece's. If you should have this item in your collection, I would appreciate hearing from you.

The above oval warmer was introduced in the 1955 Christmas catalog. In 1960 it sold for $2.25 and would later be discontinued. *Hardman Antiques.*

There is a warmer with gold decorations on it but lacking the Autumn Leaf decal. This warmer is desirable as a "go-with" among collectors. If you should have this warmer in your collection, I would appreciate hearing from you.

The above round Autumn Leaf warmer, with the original packaged candles, was introduced in 1956 and fits the 8-cup drip coffee maker or under the covered casserole. In 1960 it was selling for $2.25 and would be discontinued later that year. *Byerly Collection.*

It was only a Jewel suggestion to keep a casserole warm. The photograph above shows the round warmer used under the covered casserole. *Byerly Collection.*

Introduced in 1954, the above three-tier tidbit tray was listed as Item No., 5B42. Made of plates from the regular dinnerware line, tidbits do not have backstamps in the normal position. The 10-1/4" plate has an off-center backstamp which allows for the center handle to be placed and allows for drilling. Often referred to as an hors d'oeuvres, cookie, or candy plate, it is a two- or three-layer serving piece with a metal upright handle. *Author's Collection.*

Above "How to Assemble TIDBIT TRAY" came with the 3-tier tidbit tray. The tidbit tray's hardware was enclosed. *Byerly Collection.*

Shown above, a two-tier tidbit tray. While in the archives at Barrington, Illinois I was unable to locate any information or see documents on this piece. It is believe that it was a simple alteration of the three-tier tidbit tray. If anyone should have documentation on the above I would appreciate hearing from you. *Byerly Collection.*

The Hall Autumn Leaf Bean Pots are highly sought by collectors and are becoming expensive. The hardest to find is the one handle 2-1/4 qt. Bean Pot shown above. This Bean Pot has three gold stripes. It is uncertain when this piece was first introduced. The newer one from 1960 has one single gold stripe on the handle. *Byerly Collection.*

The interchangeable lids, for both the one handle and two handle, are different in decoration only. The lid to the two handle pot has a gold band around the lid and also on the finial, while the lid to the older one has a gold band plus an Autumn Leaf motif in the center.

Shown at right, on the left is the lid to the original one handle Hall Autumn Leaf Bean Pot. Note the motif in the center of the finial on the right, the lid to the two handle Autumn Leaf Hall China Bean Pot. Note the gold trim on the finial. Note the slight difference in the placement of the steam hole. *Byerly Collection.*

Shown above, the one handle 2-1/4 qt. Bean Pot. Note the bold and vivid coloring of the motif and gold trim. *Byerly Collection*.

Introduced in 1960, the above was a "NEW" - 2-1/4 Qt. Bean Pot. A handsome addition to your Autumn Ware line that lent a "special occasion" glow to a baked bean dinner and offered a touch of old-fashioned flavor. Listed as Item No. 5H 118, the 2-1/4 qt. bean pot sold for $3.00. By 1961 the price had increased by 25¢. *Byerly Collection.*

In 1978 a two handle Hall Bean Pot was re-issued. Variation in placement of motif can be found in Hall Jewel Autumn Leaf Bean Pot's. Some of the motif is high and some low on the bowl of the Bean Pot, shown above. *Byerly Collection.*

Of all the Hall Autumn Leaf China pieces, two sizes of butter dishes are attracting the attention of Autumn Leaf and Butter Dish collectors. The first butter dish offered in this famous motif was in 1959, and it was unfeasible. It is the wish of every collector to possess one or more of these exceptional dishes. Be prepared, they are extravagantly high priced and constantly climbing.

The 1959 deep dish covered one-pound butter shown above lasted one season. Note Crown or Regular finial. *Byerly Collection.*

Shown above a partial side view of this covered one-pound butter. Note motif on side and gold trim on finial. *Byerly Collection.*

Produced from 1961 - 1976, the above Hall Autumn Leaf (Crown finial or Regular) quarter-pound butter dish. *Byerly Collection.*

The quarter pound butter dish, shown above, was introduced in 1961 with a winged finial/handle and is definitely an Eva Zeisel design. It was designed originally for the Hallcraft line. Often referred to as a "Wings", "Quarter Pound", or "Butterfly", it can be found for one season only in the catalogues and follows the one-lb. butter and precedes the later "quarter-pounder" that remained in the line till the end. The butter dish is described in the "Jewel Home Shopping Service Woman's Catalog for Fall & Winter 1961" as "1/4 Pound Covered Butter Dish. Deep dish so butter won't slide off. Rounded cover. *5B 45 8-1/4" x 4-1/2" x 3-1/4" high and sold for $2.25". *Weales Collection.*

The (*) indicated "No Postage Charge...this item delivered by your salesman".

Wings! Wings! Isn't this an extraordinary pair? In the 1961 Fall and Winter Jewel Catalog the measurements were listed as 8-1/4" x 4-1/2" x 3-1/4" high. *Hamilton Collection.*

Shown above, the deep curve of the 1961 "Wings" butter dish underplate. *Lemons Collection.*

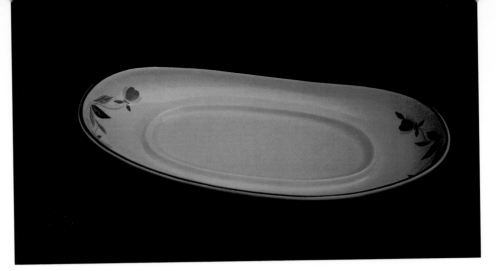

Shown above the underplate for the "Wings" butter dish. *Hamilton Collection.*

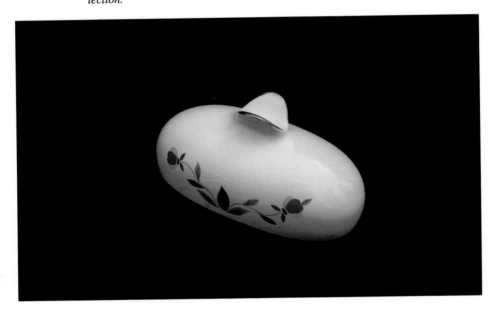

The cover of the "Wings" butter dish is shown above. Note the finial/handle, it does look like a pair of wings or a "V". *Hamilton Collection.*

Often referred to as a "smooth top grip/bar" butter dish, this dish held a quarter-pound of butter. The underplate for the above is the same as the quarter-pound "regular/crown top". Many collectors believe this was a sales award item. *Weales Collection.*

Note the "smooth top grip/bar" finial in the photograph above and the placements of the motif on the underplate. *Hamilton Collection.*

The cover and the underplate of the "smooth top grip/bar" have been separated in the photograph above to show the style of the underplate and curve lines of the cover. *Hamilton Collection.*

It is believed by some that the two "bud" one-pound butter dishes were experimental pieces submitted to Jewel; other collectors believe they were sales award. Both one-pounds have basically the same design. The only noticeable difference is in the finial base, one has the rays and the other has no rays. "Rays" describes the rays of gold at the base of the finial on top of the actual lid. Look closely at the lid to the old style 1934 sugar bowl. See the rays of gold?

Shown above, the exceptional one-pound "bud" finial butter. Note the cover, no gold rays appear at the base of the finial. *Hamilton Collection.*

The cover and underplate have been separated in the photograph above to give you a general view of these two beautiful pieces. *Hamilton Collection.*

Shown above is the underplate, which was the same style underplate for all three butter dishes. Note placement of motifs. *Hamilton Collection.*

Shown above, the backstamp of the "bud" butter dish. *Hamilton Collection.*

The 1940s Autumn Leaf bud vase, shown at left, is one of two variations. This vase has the larger decal and is commonly found. A different version of the bud vase has a smaller motif and appears to be taller than the one shown here. *Byerly Collection.*

On June 5-7, 1978 at the Jewel Home Shopping Service Convention in Las Vegas, plans were announced for a special Autumn Leaf promotion.

The promotion was the re-introduction of "pieces of the past". To ensure that the collectible value of the genuinely old pieces were not destroyed, Hall China dated "1978" on each of the pieces that Jewel was to re-introduce. At that time plans called for five pieces to be offered and the quantity was to be limited.

Sufficient stock was planned to be on hand when the offering to Jewel customers began that September. The Hall China Company had been producing pieces for Jewel to prepare for this promotion.

Shown at right, an original 1972 Autumn Leaf promotional advertisement and original captions.

'AUTUMN'...Fine Dinnerware with Coordinated Cooking and Serving Pieces

F through W — Exclusively at Jewel! **Charming 'Autumn'**, handcrafted by Hall China Company. It's semi-vitreous, extra-smooth, non-porous...guaranteed against crazing for three years! Dinnerware is thin-walled for your table. Ovenware is thick-walled for durability!

START WITH A DINNERWARE SET!
*475-0006. 16-Pc. Set. Service for Four 14.95
*475-0014. 53-Pc. Set. Service for Eight 49.95

AUTUMN OPEN STOCK PICTURED ON FACING PAGE...F through W

(F) *475-0816. 8-Cup Drip Coffee Maker 14.95
(G) *475-0618. Beverage Pitcher, 5½-pint; ice lipped 6.95
(H) *475-0667. Stacking Bowl Set (18/24/34-oz. bowls, 1 lid).......8.95
(J) *475 0733. 2-Pint Souffle/Casserole Dish 2.25
(K) *475 0725. Bean Pot, 2¼-quart 5.95
(L) *475-0774. 10-oz. Irish Coffee Mugs ....4 for 12.00
(M) *475-0790. 10-oz. Beverage Mugs ....4 for 10.40
(N) *475-0162. Covered Sugar Bowl 3.00
    *475-0196. Creamer 1.75
(P) *475-0626. 7-Cup Infuser Teapot with lift-out strainer 7.95
(R) *475-0261. Salt Shaker 1.50
    *475-0279. Pepper Shaker 1.50
(S) *475-0469. Individual Custard Cups, 7-oz. each ....6 for 4.50
(T) *475-0600. Salad Bowl, holds 3½-pints 2.50
(V) *475-0766. 12-oz. Oval Baker, for individual servings 4.00
(W) *475-0246. Gravy Boat 3.00

†Please add $1.00 for Postage and Handling
††Please add $3.00 for Postage and Handling

AUTUMN OPEN STOCK – NOT SHOWN – A wide variety to choose from, collect it all!

Item	*Cat. No.	Price	Item	*Cat. No.	Price
Cup	475-0022	1.00	Covered vegetable dish	475-0212	9.50
St. Denis cup	475-0030	1.00	Cream soup bowl	475-0287	1.75
Saucer	475-0048	.75	Ind. 10-oz. Souffle/Casserole	475-0741	4/6.00
St. Denis saucer	475-0055	.75	Divided vegetable dish	475-0303	5.00
Bread & butter, 6''	475-0063	.90	Cov. butter dish, ¼-lb.	475-0311	3.25
Salad plate, 7¼''	475-0071	.95	Covered casserole, 1½-qt.	475-0436	5.00
Pie plate, 8''	475-0089	1.00	3-Pc. Range Set (includes		
Breakfast plate, 9''	475-0097	1.35	large salt & pepper shak-		
Dinner plate, 10''	475-0105	1.75	ers plus drippings bowl)	475-0485	5.25
Small platter, 11½''	475-0113	2.00	Baking dish, 3-pint	475-0535	2.50
Large platter, 13½''	475-0121	3.00	Beverage pitcher, 2½-pint	475-0543	2.50
Fruit dish	475-0139	.90	Pie Baker, 9½''	475-0550	2.50
Cereal bowl	475-0147	.95	3-Pc. Bowl Set (1-qt., 2-qt.		
Soup-coupe	475-0154	1.45	and 3½-qt. sizes)	475-0568	8.95
Oval veg. dish, 10½''	475-0204	3.75	Pickle/Relish dish	475-0253	2.25

*No Postage Charge...this item delivered by your Area Manager

100 • JEWEL

A Jewel salesman sales card advertised "Autumn Leaf Re-issue. Complete or Add-To Your Collection! Special Offering of "AUTUMN LEAF" OPEN STOCK – Not in your Catalog." The New Autumn Leaf pieces were available from the Jewel route people only. The listing included the Cake Plate for $12.00; Cookie Jar/Bean Pot for $35.00; 10" Dinner Plate for $6.50; 7-1/4" Salad Plate; Coupe Soup Bowl for $7.50; Fruit Dish for $2.50; Cup for $3.00 and Saucer for $2.00. *Easley Collection.*

The ad listed it as dishwasher safe (because of gold banding, do not use for microware cooking). Jewel accepted either "Master Charge" or "Visa".

Buyer Beware

For many of us it is a royal treat to attend an antique show, flea market, or to browse through antique shops and auctions. We make friends with those that are established in the business. We become acquainted or familiar with numerous auctioneer. For many of those new to the world of Hall Autumn Leaf and Jewel Collecting it is easy to become a victim of misrepresentation. First learn about the collection you are about to undertake. Read any available material, inquire of the dealer or seller, and observe. It is a fact that there are dealers that provide false or misleading information.

How many time have you heard the lines, "I just bought that at an old ladies estate sale, she was 92 when she died and her house was full of Jewel", "My grandmother had that packed away in the attic", "It sells for more, but I don't want to haul it home, so I'll make you a good deal, $100 dollars, it's the best I can do", or "That's what I paid for it". The list is endless.

In a 1939 brochure promoting Jewel Biscuit Flour, and a series of recipes using the product, the display showed the perfect morning breakfast and pictured various Autumn Leaf pieces. A Madrid plate and — a very interesting idea — the 1934 creamer held syrup and the lid from the 1934 sugar bowl was used as the lid, giving you the perfect syrup pitcher, as shown below. Note — this is not a rare piece and pieces of this nature are often referred to as "mixed marriages". Beware, if you are told this is a rare piece, Jewel never offered the creamer this way! Jewel only suggested it!

The case in question! Recently I celebrated my ?? birthday. When handed a lovely wrapped gift I was told, "The man I bought this from tells me its a rare piece and I believed the price was just right, so I couldn't have passed it up". I thanked them for the lovely gift and opened the package, you be the judge of the gift I received shown at right.

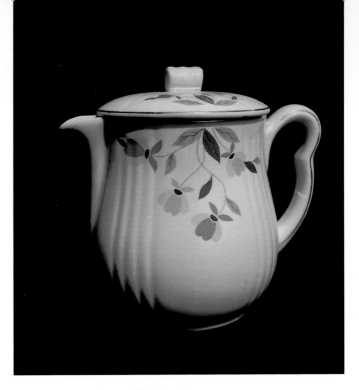

Jewel gathered together the oval metal tray, large utility bowl and six breakfast cups for a promotional coffee advertisement, in the late 1930. The advertisement suggested how to prepare a Coffee Punch. Again this was only a suggestion. Buyer Beware. The pieces are old but it not a rare set, as shown below.

Beware of Dealers passing the cake plate and nested mixing bowls off as a covered mixing bowl set, as shown above. Jewel never offered them this way! Only suggested it! *Author's Collection.*

The above wooden tray is quite useful! At one time the tray was attractive and still is. This is not Jewel Tea but a creation of some former owner. Someone has recycled a section of a plastic table cloth, cutting a section and then carefully placing the section under glass and replaced the back section. Water has gotten between the glass and the tablecloth which has caused the material to stain. *Author's Collection.*

Jewel did suggested that the Autumn Leaf paper place mats could be used in various ways. Jewel suggested to place a placemat under the glass of a tray. A tray was seen recently with the suggestion.

The pieces shown on the opposite page are quite lovely and would be a nice addition to any collection. But BUYER BEWARE!

Opposite page:
I purchased these two pieces from a local flea market, cleaned them up, and sanded them almost down to the bare metal. I purchased a can of spray paint from a local hardware store in the nearest color I could find to the Hall Autumn Leaf China. I spent a couple days carefully spraying them. I hired a local well-known artist to paint the Autumn Leaf pattern on each piece and now have a lovely kitchen set including a metal napkin holder and a metal recipe box. I could easily rough them up, price them high, peddle them at a local or out-of-state flea market, and tell some wild story.

Yes! I had the artist mark and date each piece.

There are many beautiful Autumn Leaf pieces surfacing in the secondary market and from direct mailing. Many of these pieces are made by well-known artists and designers. The majority of these pieces are well marked and the designers are developing a well known excellent name in the art world.

Not only the china, but an assortment of Autumn Leaf Clocks are available. Become aware of any piece and become acquainted or familiar with the designer before you decide to purchase that piece. Presently these pieces are moderately priced, but in the hands of the wrong person you may pay dearly.

The Autumn Leaf decal is readily available to anyone. It is easily purchased from an East coast firm with easy instructions for placing the decal on any surface. This could become dangerous in the wrong hands, and costly to a novice.

Various pieces of Autumn Leaf, shown above, were photographed for a promotional advertisement in the test kitchen in Barrington. No date appears on the back of this historical photograph. *Barrington Archives.*

Barrington invites us to breakfast served on their Autumn Leaf China. Fresh fruit served in the salad bowl, fresh Jewel coffee served in Ruffle cup and saucer, or if you prefer strong black coffee in a St. Denis cup and saucer. Hot bacon and fresh homemade waffles on the Autumn Leaf plates. Flatware used was the ever popular "Ivanhoe". *Barrington Archives.*

After the promotional photograph at right was taken, staff members might have enjoyed a light luncheon of cold cuts served on one of the Autumn Leaf platters, tomato and cottage cheese salad served on a smaller Autumn Leaf platter and a Autumn Leaf salad bowl filled with potato chips. Could the Barrington kitchen staff have been watching their weight? *Barrington Archives.*

The Barrington test kitchen offered a light luncheon in the promotional photograph below. Wedges of fresh vegetables are served in the Autumn Leaf salad bowl, possible homemade dressing served in "Radiance" custard. A fresh Summer Salad is served on a salad plate. The flatware is again "Ivanhoe". *Barrington Archives.*

113

CHAPTER 3
THE BREAKFAST SET

Table Service

An Exciting Chapter in Jewels' History, took place in 1936 when the first complete table service was to be made by "The Hall China Company".

The twenty-four piece breakfast set sold for $4.95 and included 9" plates, cups and saucers, and 5" cereal bowls which could be used as fruit bowls. A place setting is shown below. *Byerly Collection.*

At the time, this pattern had no name and was described as "ivory background complimenting the decoration which incorporates the yellow, orange, brown and rust shades of Fall". This was the first dinnerware made by "Hall" since the 1908 - 1914 era.

Hall found it necessary to invest $125,000 on the construction of a special kiln and made alterations in their factory.

The majority of artists were not under contract and were often hired by the potteries to create a specific design.

Arden Richards is believed to be the artist who created the Autumn Leaf design. It is also believed Max Hembrey, a buyer for Jewel Tea, identified/named the pattern. Max Hembrey died on September 11, 1992 at the age of 78 in Barrington, Illinois. He started working for Jewel Tea in 1935 and retired in 1974.

Once a design was selected, it was then sent to a manufacturer. Skilled lithographers in Germany actually completed the design work.

In 1935 an official from "Hall China" flew to Lakehurst, New Jersey to meet the carrier of the design. The decalcomanias/decal was aboard the Graf Zeppelin "Hindenburg" arriving from Germany. This official from Hall China returned to the East Liverpool, Ohio plant with the decalcomanias, where production began on the first table service.

A Decalcomania is the process of transferring to glass, wood, etc, decorative pictures or designs printed on specially prepared paper.

Jewel Service, 1936 Tempo!

An exciting chapter of Jewel history was being enacted as the first sets of the new Hall China dinnerware were delivered. Mr. K.K. Lilien, the assistant purchasing agent, recounted below some of the thrilling episodes of this story. Mr. Lilien is familiar with the many daring Jewel achievements of the past. He started with Jewel in 1925 as a Buffalo route manager and had been an assistant manager of the Cleveland branch and manager in Aurora, Ohio. The development of the Hall Breakfast Set, according to this veteran, ranks with the greatest of Jewel's successes.

Jewel Meets Demand For Hall China With Zeppelin, New Kiln

From the very beginning, when the first preliminary sketches of the Hall China Dinnerware were presented until the time when the first sets were loaded into freight cars, the development of the Breakfast Set has been engulfed with thrilling experiences!

Seek Quality and Distinction

When Mr. Talbot made a trip through the Northeastern part of the United States in search of the pottery manufacturer who could best make the dinnerware, his decision was The Hall China Company. Hall accepted the responsibility and made a decision to invest $125,000.00, plus hundreds of dollars more for designing and development, on the faith that Jewel sales people could sell Hall China Dinnerware in large volume.

There were months of work and much thought given to drawings, designs, and models. They made the final choice of a distinctive shape and decoration, then made the effort to get the dinnerware to the public as quickly as possible!

Jewel Service Up To The Minute

The decorations on the first sets were shipped over on the Graf Zeppelin Hindenburg. In order to get the sets to customers earlier than would ordinarily be possible, the decalcomanias were shipped on the Hindenburg.

An official of The Hall China Company flew to Lakehurst, New Jersey, where the Zeppelin landed, and was able to rush the decals back to East Liverpool, Ohio. Thus, the latest in transoceanic transportation and the latest in domestic dinnerware were not too good for Jewel and they were linked together in the Breakfast Sets.

600 Hall Workers Were Kept Busy

At that time, approximately 167,300 pieces of Jewel Hall China items were being produced each week. Approximately 600 out of the 750 Hall employees were devoting full time to Jewel orders in order to insure prompt service along with the highest quality in all shipments going to the customer. At this same time The Hall China Company placed a contract for another new decorating kiln at a cost of approximately $65,000.00.

It had been a thrilling experience to help develop this new dinnerware. However, his days on the route made one envy his even greater thrill of telling Mrs. Brown: "Did you know that the decoration on this set came from Europe on the Zeppelin 'Hindenburg'?" — K.K. Lilien, Ass't Purchasing Agent

CHAPTER 4
WORLD WAR II

Vivid Memories

World War II began in 1941 and ended in 1945. Today the name alone conjures up vivid memories for most Americans old enough to remember those years. Many were men and women who served, some who fought and died on the front lines.

There are memories of those times when many Americans did their part to help with the war by collecting, conserving and saving — Americans did their part in their own way. Scrap material was collected, rubber recycled for tires, iron and steel for guns and helmets, and paper for packaging. Rags were recycled and used for cleaning weapons and tin cans gathered together for planes. American housewives collected cooking grease that was made into explosives.

War bonds and stamps helped to pay for the war that was separated, us from the enemies, by two oceans. Nickels and dimes bought stamps which Americans filled in a book that later could be turned in for a bond.

Gasoline, some canned foods, oils, butter, cheese, beef, rubber, sugar and coffee were rationed. This was done to give everyone a fair share of scarce items.

Housewives were encouraged to use the slogan "Use it up, wear it out, make it do, or do without."

The casualties of World War II brought about a shortage of metal, resulting in metal parts and supplies being discontinued.

The above horse drawn route wagon was built in 1942 for possible use during World War II. The horse and wagon were never put into use. The back of this photograph was stamped "General Body Company", Chicago, Ill. *Barrington Archives.*

Daily Abuse

Not only the war, but daily abuse from wear of metal items caused these accessories to be in short supply. Collectors pursued metal accessories essentially in mint condition. Dents, discoloration, missing parts and pieces drastically affect the value and propensity of such piece item.

World War II shortages have resulted in current difficulties in finding mint condition examples of the metal tinware accessories associated with the Autumn Leaf line. Items that suffered due to the war were breadboxes, cake safes, canisters, cleanser cans, flour sifters, coffee dispensers, kitchen stools, thermos containers and oval trays.

Wooden

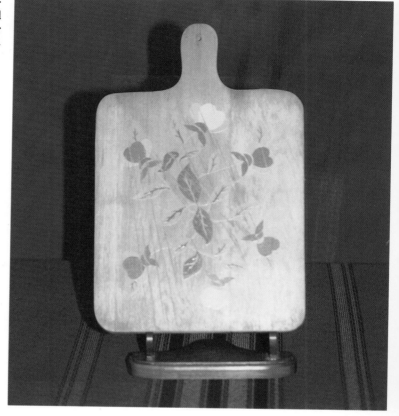

One of the most unusual Jewel Autumn Leaf items to surface is the wooden cutting board at right. The cutting board is remembered as being obtained during World War II after the owner's father had gone off to war. The owner's mother, brothers, and he were living in an apartment complex in Indiana at that time. The Jewel Tea route salesman made regular visits to the complex where they were living. During that time, the owner's mother purchased the board. The cutting board measures 7-1/2" across and 11-1/2" in length including the handle which had a hole in it for easy hanging. *Marshall Collection.*

A round wooden bowl may have been offered by Jewel during the War years. Little information is known about this unusual Autumn Leaf bowl. The bowl is part of a private collection.

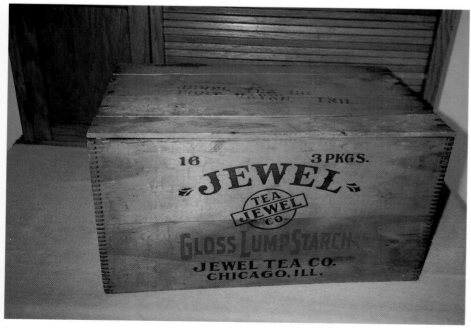

I felt that this would be a proper place to show you the magnificent Jewel Gloss Lump Starch dove tail edges wooden case at left. The height is 1' 8", and the width is 1". The top of the box is stamped Fort Wayne, In., Jewel Tea Co. The "Bar and Circle" logo appears on the side. This logo was used from 1903 to 1910. *Long Collection.*

Tinware

In 1937, to meet the requests from Jewel customers, the bread box, shown below with the conveniently open front, was introduced. Designed to fit between two shelves, the Autumn Leaf box holds three small loaves crosswise or two sandwich loaves lengthwise. It sold for $1.45 in 1938 but became one of the many metal items that was short-lived during World War II. The bread box came in a cardboard box which did not give any reference to Jewel Tea, just the Hall decoration description on the outside. The bread boxes were sold exclusively by Jewel Tea from 1937 - 1941. *Blow Collection.*

In an advertisement from Vol. 16 No. 14 of The Jewel News, 1938, the advertisement read: Matched Kitchen Ware "You'll be proud of this matched canister set and bread box in your kitchen. The modern bread box opens in front and fits between your shelves." Item No. S-1720 Bread Box, $1.45. Item No. 850, Canister Set, $1.00. Pictured were the bread box and the three canisters.

Canister Sets

The above three round graduated canisters consist of an 8-1/4", a 7", and a 6". The 8-1/4" was first introduced in 1935, followed by the 7" and 6" the following year. The 8-1/4" was introduced to hold three pounds of coffee. See "Coffee and Teapot Chapter" for other Jewel canisters. *Byerly Collection.*

Cake Safe

The Cake Safe at right (Item No.6360) had numerous uses. It could be used to store a cake, pie, or bowl of salad. It would keep food fresh longer and was great for carrying things to a picnic. In the Jewel Premium Catalog of 1941, it was listed at a bargain low price of $1.25. It first appeared in 1935; this cake safe has the Autumn Leaf decal on the top and has an attached handle for easy carrying. *Byerly Collection.*

The pamphlet shown below came with the above 1935 cake-safe. *Fausset Collection.*

JEWEL
Handle - Equipped
CAKE SAFE
Utility - Beauty - Convenience
All in One

ITEM NO. C-6360

Your friend will thank you!

Pass this booklet on to her and tell her how she can get this beautiful new CAKE-SAFE through JEWEL SAVINGS!

Recommend her to your JEWEL MAN and he will be glad to offer her the same service he is giving you.

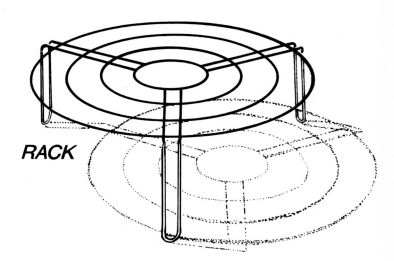

RACK

In the 1940 Jewel Premium Catalog a sturdy cake rack was offered, illustrated above. It made your cake safe do double duty. The rack doubled the capacity for shallow dishes or plates. It fit easily and snugly, listed as Item No. 1898, priced at only 20¢.

119

In November 1932 Jewel offered the above cake safe and carrier "All In One", listed as Item No. C-6118, this cake safe sold for $1.00. By December 1932, the above 3-lbs. capacity canister-dispenser was offered and listed as Item No. C-6267 and sold for 65¢. The canister measured the accurate amount of coffee for each cup. *Hamilton Collection.*

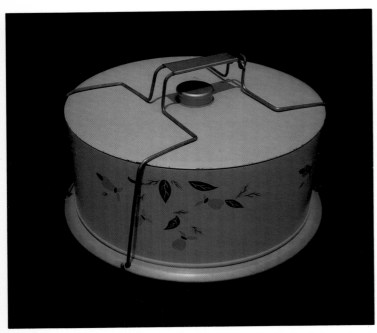

The above cake safe was introduced in 1950 and lacks the Autumn Leaf pattern on the top of the lid. This 1950 item made it convenient to carry a 2- or 3-layer cake with no danger of ruining. It was 4-1/2" deep, 10-1/2" wide, with removable wire clamps forming a carrying handle. In 1950 Hall's "Autumn" Cake Safe sold for $1.29 and was listed as Item No. 4F175. *Byerly Collection.*

Cake Safe Set. You'll be sure to want this set if you have many picnics during the summer—it is such a convenient way to carry the cake, salad or sandwiches.

Item No. C-6118	Cake Safe	$1.00
Item No. S-1440	Cake Plate	.40
Item No. C-6160	Salad Bowl	.85

The above original promotional advertisement of the Cake Safe set with captions appeared in a 1933 Jewel News. *Hamilton Collection.*

← **Safe Ladder**
A good, solid stool for the kitchen. Wooden Step Stool, Item No. 842, $2.50.

Work Is Easier →
When you sit in this Metal Kitchen Chair. Cream enamel, Hall design. Foot rest and curved back. Item No. 852, $2.75.

Prices subject to change

In the 1941 Jewel Premium Catalog the above metal chair was still listed as selling for $2.75. It was finished with baked enamel and was both attractive and easy to clean. The simple metal chair had a colorful decoration of Jewel's exclusive Hall design.

Shown at right, the Metal Kitchen Chair. The height is 2-1/2 ft., the width is 1 ft. 2 inches at the bottom. Note decal across back. *Long Collection.*

Leone Rutledge Carroll (Mary Dunbar), center, oversees refreshments served to Mrs. Julia Goddard and other Jewel employees (seated in the booth). Mrs. Bierman, housekeeper, makes adjustments to the window curtains on the right. The young lady to the left is believed to be Miss Marian Kessel. Note closely in this photograph that the lady taking notes, seated at the table, is sitting on the Autumn Leaf metal chair. Also note various metal items in this photograph, i.e. breadbox, oval metal tray, canister, metal drip and hot pads. Note carefully the many exceptional Jewel items that appear in this photograph. This historical photograph appeared on the cover of The Jewel News Vol. 17, No. 4, 1939. *Barrington Archives.*

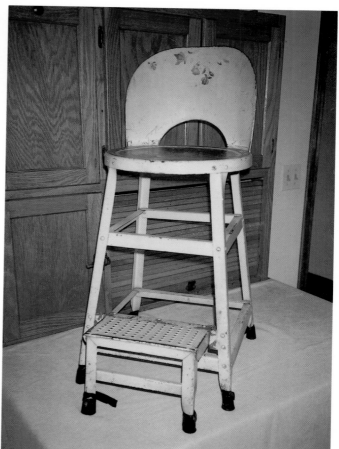

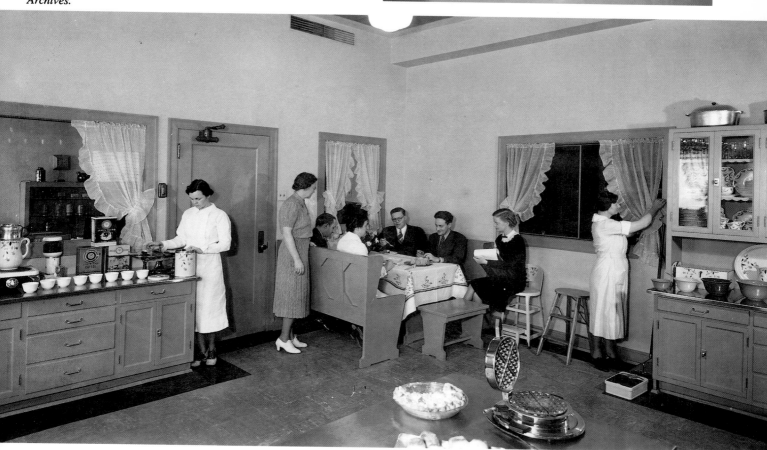

The above Cleaner Can measuring 6-7/8" high by 3-1/4" in width is another much sought after metal item. Not much is known about this war casualty due to the metal shortage of World War II. The cleaners never appeared in the Jewel catalogs as far as it is known. *Costanza Collection.*

The front view (above) of the Cleaners Can showing the Autumn Leaf pattern on both sides — the can of powder cleaner was inserted in the bottom of the Autumn Leaf Can and was secured by a wire spring clip which held it in place. Some collectors believe these came as a set. *Costanza Collection.*

Flour Sifters

Circa 1935 to 1942, the first Autumn Leaf Flour Sifter was offered, measuring 6-1/4" in height with an opening of 5". The slanted top flour sifter, shown above, is another war casualty. The wooden and metal brown grip handle is attached to the side. There is no indication as to the manufacturer. *Byerly Collection.*

Shown at right is the front view of the sifter shown above. This exquisite Autumn Leaf Flour Sifter is in exceptionally good condition. *Byerly Collection.*

Picnic Thermos

ITEM NO. 6498
ONE ONLY
ONE GALLON PICNIC JUG

DO NOT DROP
BREAKABLE
HANDLE WITH CARE

Shown above is the One Gallon Picnic Jug box, Item No. 6498. The carton contained only one picnic jug. This Picnic Jug is in exceptionally good condition. *Byerly Collection.*

Opposite page:
Very little is known about the "Autumn Leaf" Picnic Thermos bottle. It is pictured in a 1941 photograph with the metal cake safe. Note the tag on the left side of the Thermos. The back of the tag reads: For Hot or Cold Food or Beverage. It features Dual Coated Ductillite Steel, White Vitreous Clay Liner, High Efficiency Cork Insulation, Aluminum Cap and Stopper, Exclusive Vacuum Release Value, and Tap Valve for Drawing Liquid. It was manufactured exclusively for Jewel Tea Co., Inc., Jewel Park, Barrington, Illinois. *Byerly Collection.*

DIRECTIONS
READ CAREFULLY BEFORE USING
If the following directions or suggestions are closely followed, much better results in the use of this THERMIC JUG should be obtained.

TO KEEP CONTENTS HOT
To keep liquids or foods hot, the jug should be filled with boiling hot water and allowed to stand for about ten minutes, until the inside of the jug is thoroughly warmed, so that all the chill is removed. Empty this water and put in the liquid or food that you desire to keep hot. Close lid immediately.

Hot liquids should be at or near the boiling point when put into the jug, and the jug should be filled to the top, so that greater efficiency is obtained.

TO KEEP CONTENTS COLD
Fill the jug with cold water, and allow to stand ten or fifteen minutes. This should be done so that the jug will be thoroughly chilled or all the heat taken out of it. Then empty the jug and put in the contents that you desire kept cold. Close lid immediately.

To get the best results, do not expose this jug to the sun when filled with cold liquids, or set in severe wind or draft when it contains hot liquids.

According to the care given, as per above instructions, and with average external conditions, contents should hold temperature with only slight loss for from 8 to 10 hours.

The inner liner of this jug is made of earthenware. Reasonable care should be given to avoid rough handling, inasmuch as pottery is fragile.

If faucet should work tightly after use, place a few drops of oil in the inner, tapered core which will usually relieve the tendency of the two parts to stick, as a result of lime deposits or fruit acid action.

To insure a tight fit the faucet is built into the jug and is not replaceable.

This jug has been rigidly inspected before leaving the factory. It is in perfect condition and will give you many happy years of service.

JEWEL TEA CO., INC.
JEWEL PARK
BARRINGTON. ILL.

Printed in U.S.A.

The above directions were included with the "Autumn Leaf" Picnic Thermos bottle. *Byerly Collection.*

125

Trays

The lacquer finish on many of the metal accessories were easily damaged from using and washing; this reduces the value of a metal piece.

The first piece, other than Hall China, to have the Autumn Leaf design is the above 18-3/4" oval metal serving tray. The high quality lithographed tray can be found in the 1934 catalog with a complete coffee service. The tray displays the pattern at each end, with three complete lines circling the lip in one brown tone and two rust colors. By 1938 the oval metal tray was discontinued. *Author's Collection.*

The red Autumn Leaf metal tray at right is approximately 17-3/4" long and 12-3/4" wide. The design matches the wastebasket, shown at top of page 127. *Weales Collection.*

Wastebaskets

The above red Autumn Leaf metal wastebasket, is 14-1/2" high and 13-1/2" across at the top. The design matches the rectangular tray. The wastebasket is from the late 1940s - 1950s era and was marketed exclusively through Jewel Tea. *Weales Collection.*

The items were listed and promoted in August 13, 1951. They were price listed as 4F193 - Serving Tray -"Autumn" Pattern 50¢ and 4F195 - Waste-basket - "Autumn" Pattern $1.00.

There have been reports of a brown with gold Autumn Leaf design wastebasket; I have never seen one, but if you know of one or have the wastebasket, I would appreciate hearing from you.

Coaster Set

Shown at right is the 9-pc Beverage Coaster Set–Item No. S-1724A. The set includes one 7-1/8" large hot pad with a tin back and eight 3-1/4" glass coasters, not shown. *Byerly Collection.*

The cardboard carton displays various premium Hall Jewel Tea items. The carton is shown on the following page and reads as follows: 9 Piece Beverage Coaster Set, Jewel Tea Co., Inc., Jewel Park, Barrington, Ill. *Byerly Collection.*

The 9-piece Beverage Coaster Set shown below is marked Design No. 4. No mention is made of The Jewel Tea Co., Inc. which appears on the carton. The same Hall Jewel Tea items appear on this carton as those on the above Autumn Leaf 9-piece Beverage Coaster Set. The items pictured include the long-spout teapot, coffee maker and metal drip on a Autumn Leaf coaster, 6 custard cups on smaller coasters, covered 2 qt. casserole on a coaster, a flower pot on coaster and the Madrid Water Set. This same set in original packaging has been seen with a Dutch Boy and Girl on it. *Author's Collection.*

The oval Autumn Leaf gold metal backed hot pad, shown above, is 10-3/4" x 7-1/8". The backing folds around to the front, forming a narrow rim on the slick paper front. Many of these hot pads are found warped, bubbled, and stained. These hot pads were easily stained. Unable to date this oval hot pad at the present time. *Author's Collection.*

The black 7-1/4" asbestos hot pad, shown below, is somewhat hard to find. Available with the 1930s coffee service set, the back is white metal and folds around to the front, also forming a narrow rim around the asbestos. The center section of the hot pads read: THIS SIDE-UP DO NOT PUT POT ON DIRECT FLAME USE THIS PAD BETWEEN FLAME AND POT FOR KEEPING COFFEE HOT USE LOW FLAME. See "Coffee and Teapots" Chapter. *Author's Collection.*

In September 1946, the above was promoted as a "Metal Hot Pad". The popular Hall Autumn pattern is lithographed over a base cream coating to match your Hall Dinnerware. The felt-like back, shown on the right, protects the surface of a table from scratches as well as from heat. It is a convenient size, 7-3/16" across. The felt-like back came in either red or green. The number was 54094 and sold for 20¢. *Byerly Collection.*

Tins

A variety of Holiday tins, decorated coffee, tea and candy tins would appear on the open market in later years. Today collectors search for these highly decorated tins. For additional tins see "Product" Chapter.

The Holiday Fruit Cake Tins from 1981 have become a popular item among collectors. This Holiday Tins offered a 1-1/2 lb. fruit cake inside. The date is stamped on the lid at the base of the Autumn Leaf decal "JEWEL 1981". *Author's Collection.*

Jewel was proud to present a special fruit cake recipe for your eating enjoyment in 1981. The cake tin, shown below, includes the actual sealed cake still inside. The brochure included with the cake reads: "Our 1981 Jewel fruit cake recipe is a perfect blend of select nuts and fruit — pecans, dates, pineapple, cherries, and raisins. Add to this the sweet taste of honey and you have the most delectable cakes Jewel has ever offered." This tin is a tan color, as the one shown above is white. Distributed by Jewel Home Shopping Services, Barrington, Illinois 60010. *Moos Collection.*

The tin canister with a white plastic lid, shown left, is believed to have held candy. On the side near the seam appears "TM AMER. CAN CO. CANCO Reg U.S. Pat Off." On the opposite side of the seam appears the number 68-A. *Author's Collection.*

Shown below is a tan tin that could hold 24 oz. The paper label on one side reads: "J.T.'s General Store Exclusive Fruitcake and Tin. J.T's General Store is proud to present to you a fruitcake that has been specially formulated for your enjoyment. This tin was designed exclusively for J.T.'s General Store. Only a limited quantity have been made." A paper label on the bottom reads: "JT's #38-497 1-lb. 8 oz. Cake In Tin - 08055." *Author's Collection.*

The beautiful tin chest shown above held tea bags. Scripted inside the lid: "This Imported Treasure Chest Contains 150 Jewel Tea Bags 'Famous for Delightful Flavor'." In 1947 Jewel offered, among their many lovely Christmas items, this unusual Imported Tea Chest. Packed with 150 Jewel Tea bags, "famous for delightful flavor," this gorgeous tea chest made a practical, as well as a beautiful, gift. It is richly embossed and lavishly decorated in gold, red, blue and green. The Tea Chest is 9" long, 6" wide, and 4" deep. *Hedges Collection.*

Shown above is another attractive Jewel Tea Tin. A paper label appears on the lid. *Schwartz Collection.*

Shown at left is the tin J.T.'s General Store™ match holder. The top lid flap is missing; a lower lid flap covers the enclosed matches. The back is stamped: ©JASCO HONG KONG. Openings on either side allow for matches to be struck. *Author's Collection.*

Ice skaters decorate the below holiday 2 lb. tin that held the ever popular fruit cake. Around the side of the lid it reads: "Manufactured by Jewel Tea Co., Inc., Barrington, Illinois." *Author's Collection.*

The above attractive brown, gold and white tin is believed to have held candy. A white plastic lid kept the contents fresh. *Byerly Collection.*

Shown above, the 14-oz. Fruity Snack Mix tin distributed by Jewel. *Byerly Collection.*

Comb Case

The exceptional metal Comb Case, shown at the right, is 8" wide at the front and 3" deep where the combs lay, 3" from front to back and the back is 5-1/2" at the highest point. This case could be hung on a wall or a cabinet. The design around "The Jewel" located in the back is almost like the Bar and Circle logo. This is definitely an old piece. Other Comb Cases have been found with different designs in the back. There is no indication of the manufacturer of this case. *Hamilton Collection.*

CHAPTER 5

A Variety of Cookware

Jewel provided the American housewife with a variety of kitchen cookware. From the finest in aluminum ware to the most practical in enamel ware and glassware. Cookware would appear continually in various Jewel News, Jewel Premium Catalogs, and eventually Jewel Home Shopping Service Catalog.

The most popular cookware sought by collectors is those pieces that carry the famous Autumn Leaf (Flower) pattern or the Mary Dunbar Seal of Approval.

Arrow Ware Cereal Cooker

Handy, excellent quality cooker. Base capacity 3 quarts; insert 2 quarts. Made of highly polished aluminum with sun-ray interior. Not limited to cereals. Good for sauces, soft custards, puddings, in fact, any use of a double boiler. Easily handled and cleaned. Price $1.95. Our Item No. 38. Manufactured by West Bend Aluminum Co., West Bend, Wis.

Arrow Ware Safety Lid Kettle

Safety lid, 8-quart beautiful aluminum kettle. Has pouring lip. No need to burn your fingers. Lid is held stationary. Excellent for fruits, vegetables, preserves, etc. Price $2.50. Our Item No. 40. Manufactured by West Bend Aluminum Co., West Bend, Wis.

Cast Iron Skillet

"Just like grandmother used to make" will be the greeting to a dish of spring "frys" when they have been prepared in this splendid cast iron skillet. Regardless of what other frying utensils you have, an iron skillet is always a necessity. It is excellent for deep fat frying. Has two pouring lips and a well balanced handle. It is 10 inches in diameter and 2 inches deep. Price $1.15. Our Item No. 765.

This Cast Iron Skillet has come along way only to be replaced by the Microwave in today kitchens. The original 1926 Jewel News advertisement and caption is shown above.

The Arrow Ware Cereal Cooker and Arrow Ware Safety Lid Kettle, shown above, appeared in a 1926 Jewel News.

Aluminum Sauce Pan

It is a pleasure to cook fruits, vegetables and sauces in this beautiful 3-qt. pan of heavy gauge aluminum. It has rolled edges and two pouring lips, enabling the housewife to pour, holding the pan in either hand. The handle is well riveted in and is a convenient length. Price 80c. Our Item No. C-6034.

In 1926 the Jewel News listed the Aluminum Sauce Pan shown at left with the original caption that appeared in the publication.

The Arrow Ware Oval Roaster, shown below, appeared in 1926. Manufactured by West Bend Aluminum Co., West Bend, Wis.

Oval Dish Pan

A good strong, oval aluminum pan which will fit into the average sink. Easy to keep clean. Convenient family size. 12-quart capacity. Price $3.00. Our Item No. 10.

1927 Jewel News offered the above West Bend Aluminum Co., Oval Dish Pan. This is the original advertisement and caption that appeared in the publication.

The preserving Kettle and the Arrow Ware Windsor Kettle, shown below, were 1926 premiums.

When canning season arrived, most housewives turned to Jewel for their canning needs. Shown below, the original "Insure Home Canning" advertisement and caption for Fruit Jar Rubbers appeared in 1927.

Preserving Kettle

Canning season demands not only good fruit and vegetables, but also good utensils to cook them in. This 10-quart, heavy gauge aluminum kettle, with its wide bottom surface, assures uniform cooking and plenty of room for stirring. The handle is well constructed and there is a pouring lip. Price $2.10. Our Item No. 13.

Arrow Ware Windsor Kettle
Easily cleaned, durable kettle, 4-quart size. Popular design, heavy grade aluminum. Sturdy handle. Price $1.75. Our Item No. 41. Manufactured by West Bend Aluminum Co., West Bend, Wis.

Insure
Home Canning

Home canned fruits and vegetables are mighty good, but mean a lot of work. Let's make sure that none of that work goes to waste through using old or faulty rubbers. Jewel Fruit Jar Rubbers insure against spoilage. They make a tight, lasting seal, and the "two-lip" feature *is* handy in adjusting to hot jars, as well as an aid in opening them. Item No. S-1161. Price 10c.

Mary Dunbar Heat-Flow Ovenware

At one point Jewel offered customers the Mary Dunbar Heat-Flow Ovenware at no cash outlay. It was their method of advertising the delicious oven dishes you could make.

The above promotional advertisement photograph appeared in a 1938 Jewel News. At that time Jewel had finished developing recipes and had taken photographs that would appear in a recipe folder that would be packed with the Mary Dunbar Heat-Flow Ovenware. The above photograph was taken for the booklet.

The shallow custard cups with wide bases made convenient serving dishes. They had the bases made wider so that the cups would not tip in the oven or refrigerator.

The baker or shallow loaf pan. The handles had been put on the ends so it could be held without sticking ones thumb into the cake.

The loaf pan was a welcome addition to this ovenware line. The handles made it easier to handle and reduced the danger of slipping. The loaf pan was excellent for breads, molded salads, and desserts.

Scientific experiment had proven the desirability of glassware for baking pies. The heat radiation made more uniformly brown crusts and the stippled bottoms on all of these pieces were to promote ready heat penetration.

The new casserole was attractive and the knobby handles were an added feature. The flat cover could be used as a small pie plate, which made the set more complete, but was simpler than the usual cover and was easier to stack.

The large oval casserole was Mary Dunbars' favorite. In Jewel's glassware line the flat cover furnished a piece of equipment that would be used as frequently as the casserole itself. It was not only a shallow baking dish, but was also excellent as a hot platter for serving anything that was to be kept hot. The best feature was that it made a splendid steak platter.

← **Convenient Size**
For many purposes. Knobs make it easy to handle when hot. *Heat-Flow* Loaf Pan, Item No. 427, 50c.

Luscious Pies →
Can be baked and served in this transparent, easy-to-clean *Heat-Flow* Pie Plate. Item No. 422, 30c.

Printed in U. S. A.

In 1939 the promotional advertisements that appear above and in the opposite photograph appeared in a Jewel News.

← **Does Not Stain**
Ideal for Jewel-Jell salads, ice-box puddings, and cakes. *Heat-Flow* Baker, Item No. 424, 60c.

For Company Crowds →
Use it for baking and serving. Use cover in broiling meats. *Heat-Flow* Oval Casserole with Cover, Item No. 426, $1.35.

The Heat-Flow Glass Ovenware also appeared in a 1941 premium book. Foods baked more evenly in Heat-Flow and it was guaranteed against oven breakage.

Available were: the No. 422, 9-5/8" x 1-1/2" pie plate; No. 423, 1-1/2 quart covered casserole; No. 424, 10-1/2 x 6-1/2" x 2" baker; No. 425, 4 oz. custard cups in a set of six pieces; a 2-qt. No. 426 covered oval casserole; a loaf pan No. 427.

The 1-1/2 quart covered casserole is shown above. The covered lids also served a dual purpose as they could be used as a pie plate or a meat platter. By 1950 these items ceased to appear. *Author's Collection.*

The Heatflow Pie Plate, shown at right, was "Tested and Approved By Two Nationally-Known Authorities", Mary Dunbar and Good Housekeeping Bureau. *Author's Collection.*

Mary Dunbar Frypan

In 1958 it was listed as a new Mary Dunbar automatic frypan that had it's own separate thermostatic control that plugged into the pan. The 12" square frypan was streamlined in design and lightweight, with an aluminum body and a high dome self-basting cover.

Exciting New Hallite Utensils by Wear-Ever

Special Aluminum Alloy...copper-colored covers NEVER tarnish..NEVER need polishing!
Low-heat cooking...lightweight utensils spread heat 3 times faster than ordinary metals!

True Glamor with New Hallite by Wear-Ever... a utensil for every need. Extra-hard, durable alloy construction spreads heat with amazing speed...up the sides and over the cover, as well as across the bottom! The whole utensil does the cooking, over low heat without scorching or burning. Easy to keep gleaming bright...copper-colored covers never tarnish, never require special polishing. Stay-cool Bakelite handles in gleaming black have copper-colored hanging rings. Satin finish inside, mirror polished outside. Each pan and cover has its own transparent heat hanger, permitting you to hang both pan and cover on your kitchen wall. Glamorous and practical, the new Hallite will delight the homemaker.

1 – 4A 148. 2½-Qt. Sauce Pan and Cover. A basic utensil for your kitchen cooking needs!................7.45

2 –4A 150. 1½-Qt. Double Boiler and Cover. Both pans hold full 1½-qts! Inset pan has two handles.................9.95

3 – 4A 149. 1½-Qt. Sauce Pan and Cover.................5.95

4 – 4A 147. 10½" Fry Pan and Cover. Beautifully styled, it frys everything to a turn!...............9.95

5 –4A 151. 5½-Qt. Dutch Oven. Copper-colored twist handles enhance the appearance! Cover included................9.95

NEW! Patriot Ware by Revere

- Easy to Clean ● Heatlined Stainless Steel
- Heat conducting carbon steel core gives fast, even heat – heat spreads across bottom and up sides to give perfect results every time on low or medium heat
- New vapor seal construction for waterless cooking... all the precious vitamins and minerals are preserved, no cooking odors, and it helps keep kitchens cool!
- Easy to clean seamless construction. No rivets, cracks or crevices to trap food...never needs polishing

Designed for gleaming, lasting beauty... durable stainless steel with uniform heatlined centers assure tasty dishes! High dome-beaded covers (no sharp edges) are self basting, tight fitting to hold the heat and steam inside. Mirror polished outside, satin finish inside. Foods slide off the smooth, non-porous surface. "Sure-Grip" Black bakelite handles and knobs stay comfortably cool – no need to use pot holders.

1 – 4B 52. 1-qt. Covered Sauce Pan 4.95
2 – 4B 53. 2-qt. Double Boiler 10.95
3 – 4B 54. 6-qt. Covered Dutch Oven 12.95
4 – 4B 51. 10-inch Covered Skillet 9.95

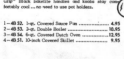

51

Mirro Aluminum

1 – Covered Cake Pan. Bake, carry, store food in one pan! For cake, meat, casseroles and salads...cover doubles as cookie sheet. Easy to carry to picnics, parties, etc. Rounded corners for easy cleaning. 4A 133. 13 x 9 x 2⅜" deep....2.95

2 – Mirro Square 'Tubed' Cake Pan. For angel food, sponge and chiffon cakes. Leak-proof, batter-seal bottom...easy to remove. Sanitite rim. 4A 141. 9 x 9 x 4" high......2.95

3 – New Mirro 3-Pc. Saucepan Set. 3 kitchen aids you can't do without! Hold 5/8, 1 and 2 quarts. Nest together to save storage space. Easy-grip handles.
4A 159...............3.10

4 – Mirro-Matic Pressure Cooker for cooking, canning. Adjust gauge for 5, 10, 15-lb. pressures; slide handles apart to open cover. Side handles on 6-qt. only. Selective control automatically prevents pressure from going higher than required. Complete with rack and recipe book.
4A 50. 4-qt. (4 pint jars).......14.95
F-4A 117. 6-qt. (7 pint jars)..19.95

5 – 5-in-1 Pan. A very versatile utensil for you to own! Use as double boiler, casserole, saucepan and sauce pot...weighted cover with fuel-saving heat indicator fits recess in either pan. 2-quart inset top; 3-quart base. Smooth, easily cleaned, rounded edges; accurate cup graduations indicated.
4A 22. 5-in-1 Pan...........3.50

Stainless Steel Ware

6 – Double Boiler. Each pan has 2-qt. capacity. Separated, both pans may be used as saucepans...cover fits both. Stay-cool handles have rings for hanging and sure grip.
4B 17. Stainless steel............7.95

7 – Covered Saucepan. Easy-clean satin finish inside; stainless stays bright without polishing. Snug cover holds flavor in. Stay-cool handle and cover knob. 1-quart capacity.
4B 15. Covered saucepan.......3.50

8 – Covered Chicken Fryer. Tight-fitting lid, stay-cool knob and easy-grip handle. Domed cover...4" deep; good for all deep fat frying...dutch oven dinners, too.
4B 18. 10½" diameter...........7.95

9 – Covered Saucepot. Easy-grip, cool Black plastic handles on each side for easy lifting, excellent balance. Snug domed cover keeps flavor and steam in. Satin finish... easily cleaned. Perfect for cooking soups, pot roasts, stews, and for making jams, jellies, and pickles. Family sized 3-qt. capacity.
4B 16. Covered saucepot........6.50

10 – Three-Piece Bowl Set...quality gauge, lasting stainless steel. Rolled lips prevent dripping rings for sure grip or hanging. Nest for easy storage. Make attractive serving bowls for popcorn, potato chips, etc. You'll find many uses for these serviceable mixing bowls. Sizes: ¾, 1½, and 3-quart.
4B 50. Set of 3 bowls.........5.95

11 – Spun Aluminum 3-Piece Range Set. Salt, pepper and drippings container. Shakers hold 5 ounces each...drippings container has 16-ounce capacity...tight fitting cover.
4A 114......................3-pc. Set 1.50

12 – Set of Four Aluminum Canisters have embossed identifying names. Spun-ray finish; polished bases and tight fitting covers...knobs are Black plastic. 6, 7, 8 and 8½" high.
4F 296..........................Set of 4 for 4.98

13 – Happy Day Four-Way Griddle Grill. It broils, grills, bakes or fries! One side is ribbed, one side is flat. Made of heavy aluminum...thicker in the center for even heating.
4A 62. Size: 10 x 11 inches.....................4.25

14 – Trig...The Singing Tea Kettle. Stainless steel with solid copper bottom. Features trigger operated spout cap.
4A 85. 2½-quart capacity..........................4.95

15 – Hallboy Water Pitcher has ice bridge and easy pouring lip; bakelite handle. Polished lightweight aluminum outside.
4A 153. 3-quart capacity.........................1.49

Jewel offered only leading manufactures of cooking ware as shown in the above advertisement with captions from 1958.

Royal Glas-Bake

In 1961 the Autumn Pattern Ovenware was listed as Royal Glas-bake "that goes from the oven right to the table for piping hot meals, and right to the freezer for cold storage." It was guaranteed against heat or cold breakage.

Listed as Item No. 4D 46, was a 2-quart round casserole with clear glas-baker cover.

Item No. 4D 47 was a 1-quart casserole with clear glas-bake cover.

A four piece bowl set was easy to hold and featured drip-free pouring. The bowls were deep, full size, perfect for mixing, baking, serving and nested for storing. Listed as Item No. 4D 49. They consisted of a 1-1/2 quart, 2-1/2 quart and a 4 quart.

A 8-1/2" x 11-3/4" x 2" deep divided vegetable dish allowed each side to hold generous portions. Listed as Item No. 4D 48.

The ovenware was not a popular item and was discounted in 1962. This ovenware is highly sought after by today's collectors. The 4 quart bowl is shown below. *Byerly Collection.*

Porcelain-Clad Cookware

Introduced in 1979 was Jewel's exclusive Autumn Flower heavy steel cookware set. The set consisted of a 1-1/2-quart and a 2-quart covered saucepan, a 5-quart covered Dutch oven and a 9-1/2" open skillet. The cover to the Dutch oven also fit the skillet. The set was heavy steel core which heats up quickly and evenly. The attractive, chip-resistant porcelain exterior wiped clean easily. They had heat-resistant handles. The covers were tight fitting which cut moisture loss to a minimum. They had convenient hang-up rings.

Shown above, the porcelain 2-quart saucepan with its lid. *Byerly Collection.*

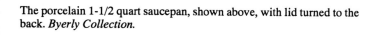

The porcelain 1-1/2 quart saucepan, shown above, with lid turned to the back. *Byerly Collection.*

Shown above, the 5-quart covered Dutch Oven with its cover. *Byerly Collection.*

Above, the 5-quart covered Dutch Oven with cover removed and laid to one side. *Byerly Collection.*

Shown above, the porcelain 9-1/2" open skillet. This porcelain ware has never been used. *Byerly Collection.*

Shown above, the 9-1/2" open skillet with the cover to the Dutch oven that also fit the skillet. *Byerly Collection.*

145

Jewel introduced the above matching 2-quart capacity teakettle at the same time. It is durable porcelain enameled metal with a heat-resistant wooden handle. *Byerly Collection.*

Introduced in 1980, the 3 piece nested mixing bowl set which was attractive enough to use for serving at any table. Made of durable porcelain enameled metal. The set included a 1.3-quart, a 2-quart and 2.6-quart size. The set originally sold for $29.99. The above photograph shows only the 2.6-quart mixing bowl. *Byerly Collection.*

Perfect for entertaining directly at any table was a 2-quart fondue set.
Chip-resistant porcelain enameled metal with wooden handle. Brown
metal cover with heat-resistant wood knob. Black iron metal stand holds
6 color-coded fork within easy reach. Chrome plated burner with brown
metal tray shown above. *Byerly Collection.*

In 1980 the 3-piece bakeware/casserole set shown left was introduced. The set featured 1-quart, 2-quart and 3-quart casseroles. The homemaker could cook, serve, and store in them. Leftovers were no problem for the set included handy plastic storage snap on lids to seal in freshness. Extended rim at each end provided easy handling. The set originally sold for $29.99. *Byerly Collection.*

The above 2-quart saucepan introduced in 1980 was of durable porcelain enameled metal with a handy pour spout and a heat-resistant wooden handle. The saucepan sold for $14.99. *Byerly Collection.*

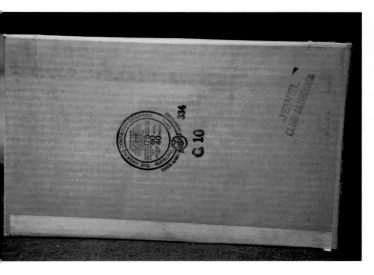

The original box for the above G10 Club Aluminum Top-Stove roaster. This roaster is in mint condition. *Hamilton Collection.*

The Club Aluminum Dutch Oven promotional photograph appeared in 1938. Note the Aluminum Coffee Pot and the Oval Serving Bowl.

Shown below, a G10 Club Aluminum Hammercraft Top-Stove roaster, Regular price was $14.80, Jewel's price was $6.95. The tag reads: "©1932 Distributed by Jewel Tea Co., Inc. Barrington, Ill." A booklet was included on how to use and care for your Club Aluminum and for further information, that was furnished on request, a customer addressed Mary Dunbar, Jewel Tea Co., Inc., Barrington, Illinois ©1933. *Hamilton Collection.*

What housewife wouldn't have enjoyed one of the finest cookware sets shown below for her kitchen. This advertisement appeared in the 1970 Spring and Summer Issue of Jewel Home Shopping Service. Note that the famous name Mary Dunbar appears with a line of 3-ply stainless steel cookware.

"Enjoy fine cooking at reasonable prices with any of these fine cooking pieces; Club Aluminum®, Mary Dunbar Stainless Steel Cookware, Coronado® Cookware and Accessories," shown below, or on the opposite side of the page select the best in bakeware, Teflon® coated mirro bakeware.

Good Taste Begins with the Best in Bakeware!

I through 5 – Teflon® Coated Mirro Bakeware. Wonderful Teflon is a work-saving bakeware lining...won't scorch or stick, and clean-up is a breeze! All you need is sudsy water and a sponge to whisk off the stickiest foods, scraping and scouring are a thing of the past! Polished aluminum outside heats fast, bakes evenly. Durable Teflon coating inside.

(1) 12-Cup Muffin Pan for muffins, cupcakes, etc.
DB 0059. Perfect for no-stick popovers!........2.59

(2) Square Griddle for no-stick frying. Heavy-gauge aluminum with stay-cool black plastic handle.
DB 0018. Size: 10¾" square........5.79

(3) Cookie Pan has wide built-in hand grip edges.
DB 0026. Size: 15½ x 10½ x 1"........3.69

(4) Bake and Roast Pan has built-in hand grip edges.
DB 0042. Size: 14 x 10 x 2"........3.99

(5) Tubed Cake Pan for angel food and chiffon cakes.
DB 0034. Size: 10 x 4½" high........3.99

6 through 11 – Smart Topaze Ovenware...styled for beauty and durability! Topaz-colored glass bakeware assures even heating for better baking. Easy to clean, too. Guaranteed oven-proof; break-resistant. Imported from France.

STARTER SET makes an ideal wedding shower gift! Consists of 2½-qt. Souffle/Oven Baker and 1½-qt. Covered Casserole.
DC 0876 X5. Save 95¢ .... $5.90 Value........*Only* 4.95

Key	Cat. No.	Item	Price
(6)	DC 0918 X5	2½-qt. Round Cov. Casserole........	$3.95
(7)	DC 0900 X5	2-qt. Oval Cov. Casserole	3.95
(8)	DC 0892 X5	1½-qt. Round Cov. Casserole........	2.95
(9)	DC 0926 X5	3-qt. Oblong Utility Dish	2.95
(10)	DC 0934 X5	3-pc. Mixing Bowl Set (7"-8"-9" ..	3.95
(11)	DC 0884 X5	2½-qt. Souffle/Oven Baker	2.95

Club Aluminum...Choice of Colors and Sun-Ray or Teflon II® Finish!

A shown in color on facing page

(A) 'Holiday' Club Aluminum lets food cook the low-heat 'waterless' way in their own natural juices...you can even roast or bake on top of the stove. Scientifically cast, heavy-gauge aluminum spreads heat quickly, evenly to sides, top and bottom. Each piece is warp and dent proof. Colorful porcelain finish outside is permanently bonded; won't stain, craze or peel. It cleans as easily as china. Heatproof handles have metal flame guards and hang-up rings. Choice of inside finishes: gleaming sun-ray aluminum or no-stick Durabond Teflon II...so tough you can use metal tools!

Open Stock – 'Holiday' with Sun-Ray Finish
State color and number: 21 Harvest Gold, 46 Avocado Green or 13 Poppy Red.

Item	Cat. No.	Price
1½-qt. Cov. Saucepan	DA 1546 X5	9.45
3-qt. Cov. Saucepan	DA 1553 X5	11.95
12" Cov. Chicken Fryer	DA 1611 X5	14.95
4½-qt. Dutch Oven	DA 1587 X5	13.95

8-Pc. Starter Set includes: 1½ and 2-quart covered saucepans, 6¾" and 10" open fry pans and 4½-quart Dutch oven. Colors: 21 Harvest Gold, 46 Avocado Green or 13 Poppy Red. State color and number.
DA 1959 X5. Sun-Ray Finish..Complete 39.95

Open Stock – 'Holiday' with Teflon II Finish
State color and number; 21 Harvest Gold, 46 Avocado Green or 13 Poppy Red.

Item	Cat. No.	Price
1½-qt. Cov. Saucepan	DA 1694 X5	11.95
3-qt. Cov. Saucepan	DA 1710 X5	14.95
12" Cov. Chicken Fryer	DA 1769 X5	18.95
4½-qt. Dutch Oven	DA 1744 X5	17.95

8-Pc. Starter Set includes: 1½ and 2-quart covered saucepans, 6¾" and 10" open fry pans and 4½-quart Dutch oven. Colors: 21 Harvest Gold, 46 Avocado Green or 13 Poppy Red. State color and number.
DA 1967 X5. Teflon II Finish..Complete 49.95

Mary Dunbar 3-Ply Stainless Steel Cookware!

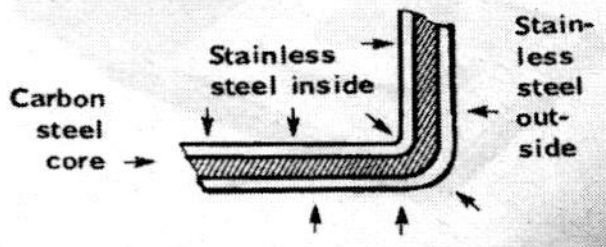

B thru G shown in color on facing page

- Mary Dunbar Cookware... for tastier meals!
- Makes an ideal gift – to give or receive!

B through G – Stainless Steel Cookware by Regal was chosen for you by Mary Dunbar for these fine quality features. Three-ply means one layer of carbon steel is bonded between two layers of extra-hard stainless steel... pans heat evenly and quickly all over; hold heat longer, too. Won't stain, pit, rust, retain odors or loose their luster. Cleans as easily as china without polishing...just wipe with a soft cloth. Flavor-sealing covers let you cook with more delicious results. Covers nest upside-down in pan so you can hang up the pan and lid as a single unit. Pans have rolled rims to make them drip-proof. Knobs and handles are of stay-cool White bakelite; teakettle has Black handle. Sleek, welded handles won't loosen or turn... handy holes for hanging to save storage space.

(B) Starter Set of 3 Covered Saucepans includes 1-qt., 2-qt. and 3-qt. sizes.
DA 1108 X5......... Starter Set 21.95
DA 1116 X5. 1-qt. Covered Saucepan........5.95
DA 1124 X5. 2-qt. Covered Saucepan........ 7.95
DA 1132 X5. 3-qt. Covered Saucepan........ 8.95

(C) Double Boiler. Cover fits top or bottom.
DA 1173 X5. 2-qt. Double Boiler........11.95
(D) DA 1140 X5. 6-qt. Cov. Dutch Oven....11.95
(E) DA 1157 X5. 10½"Cov.ChickenFryer.11.95

(F) Cooker/Steamer with colander-type inset pan. Perfect for steamed vegetables, rice.
DA 1165 X5. 3-qt. Cooker/Steamer........11.95

(G) Singing Tea Kettle. Solid copper bottom.
DA 0159. 2-qt. capacity........5.95

9-Pc. Set includes: 1-qt., 2-qt. and 3-qt. covered saucepans, 10½" open fry pan and 6-qt. Dutch oven with cover that fits fry pan.
DA 1652 X5......... 9-Pc. Set 39.95

The Prettiest Cookware Ever... Coronado is Porcelain-Clad!

H, J & K shown in color on facing page

H, J & K – Coronado Cookware & Accessories add the decorator touch to your kitchen! As practical as it is beautiful...colorful paisley-decorated deluxe porcelain enamel finish covers a heavy-duty steel base. Non-porous; surface cleans as easily as china. All pans and covers feature 18/8 stainless steel rims to prevent chipping on edges. Cooks as good as it looks...even heat distribution is assured on gas or electric ranges. Stay-cool bakelite handles and knobs with stainless steel flameguards. Detergent and dishwasher-proof. Finest imported quality; from Spain. Cookware and accessories both come in choice of Brown or Avocado paisley design on White.

(H) 8-Pc. Gourmet Cookware Set consists of: 8-in. open skillet, 10-in. open skillet, 1½-qt. covered saucepan, 3-qt. covered saucepan (cover fits 8-in. skillet) and 5-qt. Dutch oven (cover fits 10-in. skillet). Choice of: 53 Brown Paisley or 46 Avocado Paisley.
DA 1991 X5. State color & number.... Set 39.95

(J) Set of 4 Canisters. Graduated sizes to hold flour, sugar, coffee, tea, etc. Colors: 46 Avocado Paisley or 53 Brown Paisley.
DD 1071 X5. State color & number.... Set 14.95

(K) 3-Qt. Whistling Teakettle. Your choice of: 46 Avocado Paisley or 53 Brown Paisley.
DA 2007 X5. State color & number........ 9.95

All items on this page delivered by your salesman...No Postage Charges!

Cooking's A Pleasure with Easy-Care Utensils!

A Club Aluminum

Three Decorator Colors!
with choice of Sunray Polished Aluminum
or Durabond® Teflon II finish inside!

Avocado

Harvest Gold

Poppy

B — Saucepan Set

C

D

E

F

G

Mary Dunbar

H

Coronado Gourmet Cookware

Choice of Colors!

J

K

Jewel • 71

151

CHAPTER 6
NONHALL AUTUMN LEAF

At one time the Autumn Leaf decal was not exclusively for The Jewel Tea Company and could be found on various pieces made by other major pottery manufacturers of dinnerware during the 1920s and 1930s. Companies known to have produced pieces with the now famous Autumn Leaf decal include: Crooksville China Company, Columbia, Crown, Harker, American Limoges, Paden City and Vernon of California.

Numerous Autumn Leaf pieces were manufactured by a firm in Japan; there is no known information about this company at the present time. These pieces are shown at the end of this chapter.

One of the most unusual pieces is an Autumn Leaf candy dish/compote marked "Germany". A photograph of this piece appeared in a June 1983 issue of "The Glaze".

Shown below is an unusual red bail handle teapot with a yellow finial and spout incorporating the Autumn Leaf motif throughout. The teapot was purchased at a flea market seven or eight years ago. *Beguhl Collection.*

The teapots backstamp shown above resembles a flower with leaves enclosed in a shield with the letters BB below the shield, with the numbers 2157 and 4377 below the BB. The number 145/3 also appears on the bottom. *Beguhl Collection.*

One of the most extensive collections of Non-Hall Autumn Leaf presently known to exist is that of Mr. and Mrs. Larry Fausset of Tulsa, Oklahoma. The Faussets began collecting Non-Hall Autumn Leaf in 1985. After seeing the beauty and vivid colors of these pieces, they began to build the extensive collection they now own. Earlier decals are bolder and much more colorful with a greater amount of vivid oranges and browns.

Mrs. Fausset points out that the condition of the items doesn't play a big part in this aspect of the collecting. Pieces in mint condition sell for astronomical prices; however, even damaged Non-Hall pieces still command a much higher price than their Hall Autumn Leaf counterpart.

Paden

Founded in 1907 by George Lasell, Paden City Pottery was a large manufacturer of good grade semi-porcelain dinnerware. Collectors noticed right away that the Paden City ware decals looked as though they were handpainted china. Paden City Pottery, near Sisterville, West Virginia, was chartered on September 15, 1914. Principal offices were located in Paden City, West Virginia. The company was dissolved on November 12, 1963.

Papoco (PAden city POttery COmpany) markings are often found on the back side of the Paden City Pottery Company's ware.

Shown below, the backstamp on Paden Bakserv. *Fausset Collection.*

Pictured below is a 11" x 11" square Paden Bakserv plate with an orange/rust trim. *Fausset Collection.*

The paper label shown below appears on items which have both Paden Bakserv and Papoco backstamps. *Fausset Collection.*

The 11" x 11" square plate shown below is marked Paden Bakserv with no trim. Many Paden pieces were never trimmed. *Fausset Collection.*

153

Another 11" x 11" square plate shown below has the orange/rust trim and is also marked Paden Bakserv. *Fausset Collection.*

The Paden Bakserv 11" x 11" square plates below are shown for decal variation. *Fausset Collection.*

The 9-1/2" diameter x 1-3/4" high pie plate below is trimmed in orange/rust and marked Paden Bakserv. *Fausset Collection.*

Below are Paden pie bakers. The one on the left has no trim and is 9-1/2"
in diameter x 1-7/8" high. The one on the right has the orange/rust trim
and measures 8-7/8" in diameter x 1-1/2" high. *Fausset Collection.*

Papoco 9-1/2" x 9-1/2" square plate is shown below with the orange/rust
trim and embossed design around the edge. *Fausset Collection.*

The 9-1/2" square plate below is marked Papoco and also has a paper
label. It has an embossed design around the edge but no color trim. *Fausset
Collection.*

A Papoco 8-1/2" square plate is shown below with the orange/rust trim and embossed design around the edge. *Fausset Collection.*

Unmarked custard cups, below, are believed to be Paden and measure 3-3/8" in diameter x 2-1/2" high. Both without trim are shown for decal comparison. *Fausset Collection.*

Also, unmarked custard cups shown below are believed to be Paden Bakserv, measuring 3-3/8" in diameter x 2-1/2" high. The one on the left has the orange/rust trim and the one on the right has no trim. *Fausset Collection.*

The custard cups below show another variation of decals and are believed to be Paden. They measure 3-3/8" in diameter x 2-1/2" high; both have the orange/rust trim. *Fausset Collection.*

Two 6 cup Paden Bakserv Boston teapots, below, are 9-1/2" from handle to spout and 4-3/4" high. The one on the left is trimmed in orange/rust and the one on the right has no trim. Note the variation of the decals on these two teapots. *Fausset Collection.*

A Paden 2-quart water pitcher with orange/rust trim is shown. It measures 8" from spout to handle and is 7-5/8" high. *Fausset Collection.*

Below are two Paden Bakserv casseroles, the left one is a 1-3/4 quart casserole, with no trim, measuring 8-1/4" in diameter x 3-5/8" high. The one on the right is a 1 quart casserole that has orange/rust trim, measuring 7-3/8" in diameter x 3-1/8" high. *Fausset Collection.*

Below is a Paden chocolate pot with silver trim. It holds 1 quart and measures 7-3/4" high and 8-1/2" across from spout to handle. *Fausset Collection.*

Two Paden nested mixing bowls, below: the left one measures 6" in diameter x 2-3/4" deep, the right one 5-1/8" in diameter x 2-1/4" high. *Fausset Collection.*

Crooksville

On January 9, 1902, S.H. Brown, W.H. Brown, W.J. Tague, A.P. Tague and G.E. Crooks, all businessmen in Crooksville, Ohio, petitioned the Ohio Secretary of State to grant them an option for "The Crooksville Art Pottery Company". Their purpose was to manufacture a line of artware and stoneware.

On January 20 of the same year, the first stockholders met and elected officers with J.L. Bennett as President; J.M. French, Vice President; Secretary/Treasurer and General Manager, G.E. Crooks. At that time the board amended the articles of incorporation and changed the name from "Art Pottery Company" to "Crooksville China Company". After choosing a plant site, ground was broken and work began on construction in March 1902.

At one time 300 people were employed in the Crooksville Company, and an annual production of over 600,000 dozen pieces of ware were produced. Crooksville's China Company closed in 1959 after fifty-seven years in the china business. Crooksville Non-Hall Autumn Leaf is not marked but is easily recognized after one becomes familiar with the shape.

In a December 1931, issue of "Needlecraft" magazine a bargin offer was introduced to readers. The advertisement read in part, "Anyone who really wants a new dish set can have it without taking a cent from the family purse" and displayed a set of Au-tumn Leaf china decorated in a soft creamy yellow with a spray of conventional flowers in autumn browns and gold and a band of borders in a deep green shade. Notice that the deep green border appears almost black. In this section the border is referred to as black.

The set was American made with a semi-porcelain body and a glazed finish. A set for everyday hard usage was still attractive enough to put before the minister when he arrived for dinner. Safe, quick delivery was prepaid by Needlecraft. Free replacements were provided for any broken pieces.

The offer was open to anyone who read the advertisement. "Just by sending twenty, two-year subscriptions to 'Needlecraft' at 50¢ each, each subscriber would receive the magazine for two years, and you would receive this 50-piece dish set. Mention Gift No. 4007."

Every set of the Autumn Leaf pattern china contained the following pieces: 6 bread and butter plates, 6 desserts, 6 pie plates, 6 dinner plates, 6 saucers, 6 cups, 6 oatmeal, 1 - 11-1/2" meat platter, 1 - 7" covered casserole, 1 deep cereal, 1 sugar, 1 - 8" round nappy and 2 covers. This china was produced by the Crooksville China Company of Crooksville, Ohio

Right, a Crooksville platter with gold trim measures 13-3/8" x 9-3/4" x 1-3/8" high. *Fausset Collection.*

The Crooksville platter at left measures 11-3/8" x 7-3/4" x 1-1/8". *Fausset Collection.*

159

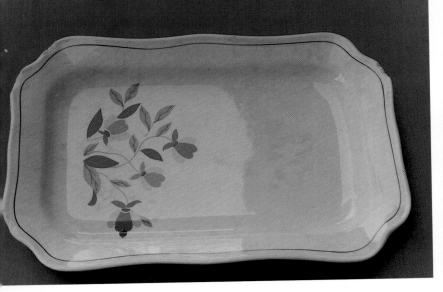

The above Crooksville platter measures 11-3/8" x 7-3/4" x 1-1/8" deep. Note the placement of the decal in both photographs. *Fausset Collection.*

Above is a Crooksville square 8-3/4" dinner plate with gold trim. *Fausset Collection.*

Above is a Crooksville 8-5/8" square dinner plate with black trim. *Fausset Collection.*

Above is a Crooksville 6-3/4" dessert plate and a 6-1/8" bread and butter plate. *Fausset Collection.*

Above are two Crooksville dessert bowls; note the placement of the decals. The bowls measure 5-1/2" x 5-1/2" x 1-3/8" deep. *Fausset Collection.*

Shown above are two Crooksville bowls. The one on the left is a soup bowl measuring 7-3/8" x 7-3/8" x 1-5/8" deep. On the right is an oatmeal bowl measuring 6-1/8" x 6-1/8" x 1-3/8" deep. *Fausset Collection.*

Above is the Crooksville cup and saucer set. *Fausset Collection.*

Shown above is the Crooksville gravy boat, which measures 8" from spout to handle, 3-3/8" wide and 3" high. *Fausset Collection.*

The above deep Crooksville cereal bowls are shown for decal variation. Each measures 6-1/8" x 6-1/8" x 2" deep. *Fausset Collection.*

Above is the Crooksville sugar with lid and creamer. *Fausset Collection.*

The above photograph shows the Crooksville covered vegetable casserole with the lid removed; below is the Crooksville covered vegetable casserole with lid. The covered casserole measures 8-5/8" x 8-5/8" x 4-1/4" deep. *Fausset Collection.*

The photograph above shows a Crooksville open nappy, often referred to as a round vegetable bowl, measuring 8-3/8" x 8-3/8" x 2-7/8" deep. *Fausset Collection.*

Vernon Kilns

The pottery started in 1916 and, until 1928, was called Poxon China, Ltd. From 1928 to 1948 the name was Vernon Potteries. It was acquired by Metlox Potteries in 1958 and ceased production in 1960.

Most of the Vernon Autumn Leaf had no trim, but occasionally a piece with silver trim will be found.

Shown below, a Vernon 16" x 11-3/4" oval platter. *Fausset Collection.*

Shown below, a Vernon creamer measuring 4-3/4" x 4-1/8" x 2-5/8". *Fausset Collection.*

The 7" x 7" saucer shown below may be a liner for a soup bowl. Note the silver trim. *Fausset Collection.*

A 10-1/8" dinner platter and a 7-3/8" bread and butter plate are shown below. *Fausset Collection.*

Shown below is an 8" diameter x 1-1/2" deep soup bowl on the left and on the right a 5-1/8" diameter x 1-1/8" deep berry bowl. *Fausset Collection.*

Shown below on the left is a silver trim 6" saucer and on the right, without trim, a 6-1/4" saucer. *Fausset Collection.*

Columbia

Columbia Chinaware was a sales organization owned by The Harker Company and operated by Harker. Columbia was in business from circa 1935 to 1955. The Harker Company was begun in 1840 by Benjamin Harker. After his death, Benjamin's sons took over the operation of the family's rather new business. In 1931, the company relocated to new quarters in Chester, West Virginia across the river from the East Liverpool site. The Jeanette Glass Company purchased Harker and closed the company in March 1972.

Above is a 1-3/4" quart capacity 8" high "tall boy pitcher" with lid; it measures 8" from spout to handle. *Costanza Collection.*

The "tall boy pitcher" with lid removed is shown above. Note the design on the lid. *Costanza Collection.*

Shown above is a handled tumbler measuring 3-1/4" in diameter x 4-1/8" high. *Fausset Collection.*

The above view of the tumbler on the left is shown for the red mark on the handle and is identical to the one on the right. This piece is not marked but is unmistakably Columbia. *Fausset Collection.*

The dinner cup and saucer set are shown above. The cup measures 3-7/8" in diameter and 2-3/4" tall; the saucer is 6" in diameter and 1" high. *Fausset Collection.*

Columbia plates is shown above; the plate on the left is 9" square and the one the right is a 6-1/2" square bread and butter plate. *Fausset Collection.*

A Columbia 5-1/2" diameter x 1-3/8" deep berry bowl is shown above. *Fausset Collection.*

A fluted 6-5/8" diameter x 2-1/2" deep serving bowl is shown above. *Fausset Collection.*

The above Columbia oval vegetable bowls can be nested inside one another. The left one is 10-1/2" x 7-1/2" x 2-1/8" high, and the right one measures 8-1/4" x 6-1/2" x 1-7/8" high. *Fausset Collection.*

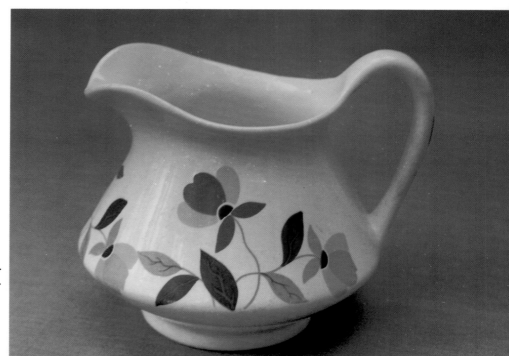

Shown right is a Columbia creamer measuring 5" from spout to handle and 4" high. *Fausset Collection.*

Shown above is the Columbia pie baker, 9" in diameter x 1-5/8" deep. *Fausset Collection.*

Above is a Columbia casserole with red trim, 7-3/4" in diameter and 4-5/8" high. *Fausset Collection.*

The Columbia 3-piece stack set at right with lid is 6-1/2" in diameter and 6-1/2" high. *Fausset Collection.*

Above are Columbia large canisters with red trim. Note the variation of the decals on the canisters. Each measures 6-1/2" in diameter and 5-3/4" high. *Fausset Collection.*

Shown above are small red-trimmed 6-1/2" in diameter and 4-3/4" tall canisters. Note how the decals differ on these two canisters. *Fausset Collection.*

Columbia canisters are shown above with red trim. The larger one measures 6-1/2" in diameter and 5-3/4" high. The smaller one measures 6-1/2" in diameter and 4-3/4" high. *Fausset Collection.*

Columbia custard cups are shown above with red trim inside the rim, measuring 3-1/2" in diameter and 2-1/2" deep. *Fausset Collection.*

The Columbia small nested mixing bowls are shown above with red trim inside of rim. The large bowl is 6-5/8" in diameter and 4" high. The medium one is 5-3/4" in diameter and is 3-1/2" high. The small bowl is 5-3/8" in diameter and 3-1/4" high. *Fausset Collection.*

The nested Columbia mixing bowls shown above are hard to find in a complete set. The large bowl measures 11-1/4" in diameter and is 5" high. The medium bowl is 10-1/4" in diameter and is 4-3/4" high. The small bowl is 8-7/8" in diameter and is 4-1/4" high. *Fausset Collection.*

Limoges

Limoges China Company of Sebring, Ohio was in business from 1900 until a little after 1955, at which time the company went into bankruptcy. It was first called Sterling China; then the name was changed to Sebring China Company. They became known as Limoges China Company. The name had been changed again because the E.H. Sebring China Company was also called Sebring China Company.

Limoges China Company was threatened with a lawsuit by the Limoges Company in France over the name "Limoges" in the late 1940s. Then the company started calling their wares American Limoges. In advertisements, etc., the company name became American Limoges China Company.

During the 1940s, Salem China Company, Sebring Pottery Company, and Limoges China Company were all under the same management.

In August 1979 it was reported that a collector had in her collection an ivory covered Autumn Leaf cheese dish made by the Limoges China Co., Sebring, Ohio. The whereabouts of this piece is presently unknown. Anyone with information about this cheese dish is asked to contact the author or Mrs. Fausset.

The Limoges China Co., Sebring, Ohio, backstamp is shown above. *Fausset Collection.*

The Limoges China Co's. "Golden Glo Ware" backstamp is shown below. *Fausset Collection.*

The Ivory cup and saucer set shown below is trimmed in silver. The cup measures 3-3/4" in diameter and 2-3/8" deep. The saucer is 5-7/8" in diameter. *Fausset Collection.*

The dinner cup and saucer set shown on the right has the "Golden Glo Ware" backstamp. The cup is 3-3/4" in diameter and is 2-3/8" deep. The saucer is 6" in diameter. *Fausset Collection.*

The 9-1/4" diameter plate and 6-1/4" diameter bread and butter plate with orange trim are shown at left. *Fausset Collection.*

Shown on the right are a 6-1/4" diameter bread and butter plate and a 5-1/8" diameter berry bowl with orange trim. *Fausset Collection.*

Shown on the left is an oval 11-5/8" x 9" orange trim platter. *Fausset Collection.*

173

The Sugar and Creamer set is shown below with orange trim. The sugar bowl is 6" across from handle to handle and 4-3/4" high. The creamer is 5-7/8" from handle to spout and 3" high. *Fausset Collection.*

Shown below are two round serving bowls that are decorated with orange trim. The left one measures 8-7/8" in diameter and is 2-1/2" deep. The right one is 8-3/4" in diameter and is 1-3/4" deep. *Fausset Collection.*

The large serving bowl shown below measures 8-7/8" in diameter and 2-1/2" deep. *Fausset Collection.*

Crown

Established by A.M. Beck, Crown Pottery began in 1882. After the death of Mr. Beck in 1884, the pottery was sold to Bennighof, Uhl and Company, who began to manufacture whiteware. By 1891 the pottery was organized as Crown Pottery Company by the Fientke family.

In 1902, Crown took over the Peoria Pottery Company of Peoria, Illinois and the two assumed the name of Crown Potteries Company. By 1904 the Peoria company was closed. Crown went out of business between 1954 and 1958. Shown below is the Crown backstamp. *Fausset Collection.*

Shown below are Crown Jugs, all with black trim. From left to right the large jug measures 7-1/2" high to the top of the lid, 9-3/8" across from handle to spout; the medium jug is 5-1/4" high without the lid, 7-3/4" from handle to spout. The small syrup is 5-1/4" high to the top of the lid and 6" across from handle to spout. *Fausset Collection.*

Below are two Crown jugs with lids and black trim like those shown above. Shown for detail of the lids. *Costanza Collection.*

Below is a 9" Crown plate with black trim. *Fausset Collection.*

The square vegetable bowl trimmed in black, shown below, is 8-1/2" x 8-1/2" x 2-1/2" high. *Fausset Collection.*

Unmarked Autumn Leaf

The manufacturer of the pieces shown below are unknown at present. For those pieces believed to be manufactured by any certain company, the company's name has been given.

Unmarked, but believed to be a Harker piece, the cake plate below measures 12" from handle to handle. Note the silver trim. *Fausset Collection.*

Shown below are an unmarked cake plate and pie lifter. Both are trimmed in silver and are definitely believed to be Harker. The plate is 12" x 10-3/4". The pie lifter is 9-1/8" x 2-1/2" at the widest point. *Fausset Collection.*

Both pieces shown below are unmarked pie lifters. Mrs. Fausset is sure they were made by Harker. She believes the larger one in front is a pie lifter and the other one is used for cake. The pie lifter measures 9-1/8" long x 2-1/2" and has silver trim; the other one measures 9-3/8" x 2-7/8" and has gold trim on the handle. *Fausset Collection.*

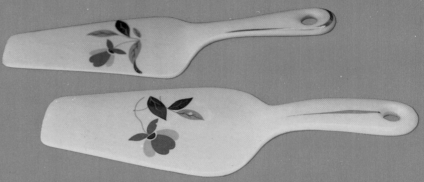

Below is an oval unmarked 11-3/4" x 8-3/4" x 7/8" high platter with gold trim. *Fausset Collection.*

Shown on the right is an unmarked 9-3/16" in diameter silver-trimmed plate. *Fausset Collection.*

Unmarked nested bowls are shown below. Each bowl has a red trim on the rim and around the middle. The bowl on the left measures 11-5/8" in diameter and 5-1/4" high. The bowl on the right is 10-3/4" in diameter and 4-3/4" high. *Fausset Collection.*

The nested unmarked bowls shown below are believed to be Harker. Each bowl is trimmed in orange. In order from left to right the measurements are 11-3/4" in diameter x 5-1/2" high; 10-3/4" in diameter x 5" high; 9-3/4" in diameter x 4-5/8" high. *Fausset Collection.*

The 10" round divided vegetable bowl shown below has silver trim and is 2-5/8" deep. *Fausset Collection.*

The unmarked lids shown below are: on the left 3-1/2" in diameter with an opening 2-3/8" and a 5/8" rim — note the orange - rust trim. Next is a 7-1/2" diameter casserole lid with gold trim believed to be Paden. *Fausset Collection.*

Japanese Autumn Leaf

Little is known about the Japanese Autumn Leaf pieces shown below. At present we are unable to ascertain the year of production. Anyone with information about these pieces is asked to contact the author or Mrs. Fausset.

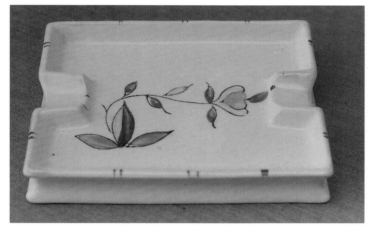

The above ashtray is 4-3/8" x 3-3/8" x 3/4". *Fausset Collection.*

The above square table set includes a 1/4 lb. covered butter dish, salt and pepper shakers, sugar and creamer. All pieces rotate on a Lazy Suzan. The base measures 7" x 7" x 2". *Fausset Collection.*

Shown above, a 3 legged 4-cup teapot with a bail handle, 5-1/4" high x 6-5/8" from spout to handle. *Fausset Collection.*

The canister set above includes a flour container 5-7/8" x 5-7/8" x 7" high, a sugar container 4-7/8" x 4-7/8" x 6-1/8" high, a coffee container 4" x 4" x 5-1/8" high and a tea container 3-1/8" x 3-1/8" x 4" high. *Fausset Collection.*

The 6-piece condiment set, above, rotates on the wire rack; it is 7" in diameter x 3" high. The set includes a covered sugar, creamer, salt and pepper shaker, and two covered condiment containers. *Fausset Collection.*

The 9-piece spice rack shown above measures 9" x 6-7/8" x 2-1/4" deep. The set includes a wooden holder with two china drawers. It also includes a pepper, salt, allspice, ginger, paprika, and cinnamon shaker. *Fausset Collection.*

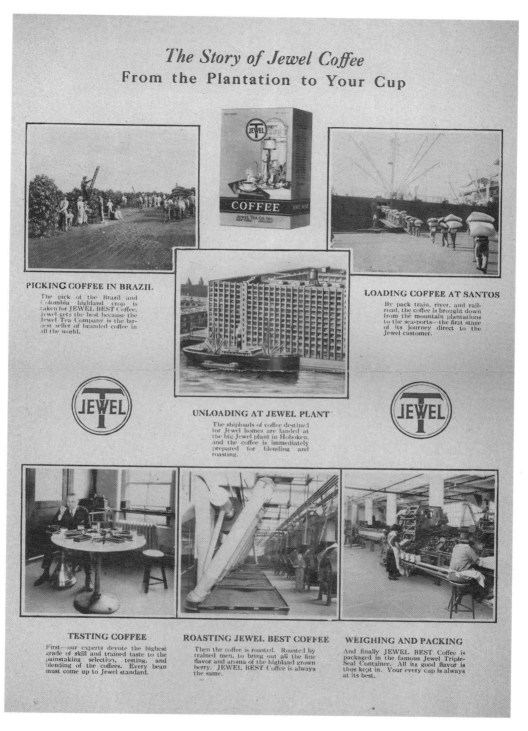

The above original document, "The Story of Jewel Coffee", appeared in a September 1925 Jewel News. The in-depth captions are shown on page 182. Note logo/trademark in the above article.

The Story of Jewel Coffee From The Plantation To Your Cup

"*Picking coffee in Brazil*. The pick of the Brazilian and Colombian highland crop is gathered for Jewel's Best Coffee. Jewel gets the best because the Jewel Tea Company is the largest seller of brand coffee in all the world. *Loading Coffee At Santos*. By pack train, river, and railroad, the coffee is brought down from the mountain plantations to the seaports — the first stage of its journey to the Jewel customer. *Unloading At Jewel Plant*. The ship loads of coffee destined for Jewel homes are unloaded at the big Jewel plant in Hoboken, New Jersey. Then the coffee is immediately prepared for blending and roasting. *Testing Coffee*. First, Jewel experts devoted the highest quality of skill and trained taste to undergo the painstaking selection, testing, and blending of the coffees. Every bean must come up to Jewel's standard. *Roasting Jewel's Best Coffee*. Then the coffee is roasted to bring out all the fine flavor and aroma of the highland grown berry. JEWEL BEST COFFEE is always the same. *Weighing and Packing*. Finally JEWEL BEST COFFEE is packaged in the famous Jewel triple-seal Container. All of its good flavor is thus kept in the coffee. Every cup is always at its best."

The above illustration from a 1926 - 1927 Jewel calendar housecard shows "The Jewel Plant on New York Harbor" (top illustration) and "The Jewel Plant in Chicago" (lower illustration). *Preo Collection*.

Shown above, in the Jewel Test Kitchen with Jim O'Conner (coffee expert and buyer) on the left, Mary Dunbar, a staff member believed to be Mavis Galloway and an unknown gentleman at the right. The photograph is dated November 18, 1929. *Barrington Archives*.

Introducing "JEWEL BEST" Coffee

In 1923, the name was changed from the original J.B. (Jewel Blend) to "Jewel Best", but remained the same highest quality coffee that Jewel had supplied to customers for years.

"Jewel Best" was specially selected and blended from the choicest coffees grown in Brazil and Colombia. Every pound conformed to Jewel's most rigid standard of quality, delicious flavor, wholesome strength, and rich aroma before it was pronounced worthy to bear the "Jewel Best" brand.

Jewel's coffee experts devoted all their time to testing and blending coffees in order that the highest standard could be maintained. The roasting was done with the largest and most modern coffee roasting equipment in the world. With the most scientific roasting methods used, this coffee always tasted the same. It retained every particle of the strength, flavor and aroma nature had stored in the highland grown berry.

"Jewel Best" was the most economical coffee a customer could buy. One pound could make forty cups of delicious beverage, of proper strength, excellent flavor, and pleasing aroma. This was, by far, more than anyone could get from a pound of ordinary coffee.

In 1923, Jewel again led the field! Not only supplying the highest quality of coffee, but "Jewel Best" was delivered in an attractive "Triple-Seal Package". A parchment bag around the coffee, then a heavy, sealed cardboard box, that was wrapped in an air-tight label. This insured fresh, clean coffee with all its natural flavor, strength and aroma. Triple-Seal prevented the coffee from becoming stale. It kept moisture and foreign odors away. The parchment bag (inner seal) prevented the oil of the coffee from soaking through the package and being lost. Jewel believed "Nothing good can get out — nothing bad can get in".

The Triple-Seal Packaging of the coffee was done entirely by automatic machinery. From the time "Jewel Best" coffee left Brazil until it arrived on a table, it was untouched by human hands. The savings, which Jewel made in the cost of packaging by automatic machinery, Jewel returned to the customer in this new package.

The "Triple-Seal Package," in which Jewel packaged their teas and coffee, was the most recent scientific development in packages, and Jewel was the first to use it. Jewel predicted that the Triple-Seal Package was the type of container which in the future would be the standard, not only for coffee or tea, but for all high grade packaged grocery articles. "Jewel Best" coffee was packaged in America's best package.

In January 1930, Mary Dunbar made a New Year's resolution and shared it with The Jewel News readers. She wrote that everyone makes resolutions for the New Year and that Jewel was no exception, including the Jewel "Home Service" staff. The staff resolved to do everything in their power to be of greater service to the thousands of American homemakers whom they called "customers." She pointed out that the Division was called "Home Service" because their principal function was to be of service to the homes in which Jewel products were used. She wanted Jewel customers to feel free to call upon them, asking for help with the many little problems which might come up in connection with their daily tasks as homemakers.

She noted one service in particular which the staff would especially like to give in 1930, and that was in connection with the movement for better coffee making in every home. Everyone accepts the fact that the two principal essentials in serving good coffee are: first to buy a good coffee, and second to make it correctly. She indicated that the company takes care of that first prequisite through offering Jewel customers nothing but good coffee, three splendid blends, and each one to meet certain tastes. Each is a blend of fine quality, zealously maintained by their coffee experts. She wrote about the part "Home Service" played in connection with the second rule — namely, make it correctly. The staff of Home Economics experts were constantly at work in the Home Service kitchen, testing the standards of Jewel grocery and premium items, working out household problems, and developing new recipes.

In a Jewel publication, Mary Dunbar pointed out a busy staff at work. The promotional photograph gave an idea of the numerous activities, a staff member mixing up a cake, another comparing Jewel Macaroni with another brand, a third testing a toaster, a fourth working with the Mary Dunbar Cooker developing new recipes for its use. At the extreme right, a coffee test was in progress with the exact weight of coffee being measured for the purpose.

She indicated the considerable amount of time which was spent in research work in order to determine the very best way to make coffee and to develop steps which Jewel customers could follow in order to have a properly brewed beverage. There were three principal methods of coffee making which any one, if these three principle methods were followed, would produce good results. She asked if the reader was having trouble when making coffee, advising that they should write to the Home Service Division, telling which method they preferred to use (pot, percolator, or drip method) and the Home Service Division would give individual help with the problems.

Regardless of the particular coffee making methods followed, the Jewel Home Service staff set down certain rules by which a customer should always comply: "(1) Keep the coffee in a tightly covered glass container. This helps to retain the freshness. The ideal thing is to buy bean coffee and grind only enough for each meal, as you are ready to use it. (2) Measure both the coffee and the water. A hit or miss method is bound to lack uniformity in results. (3) Do not over-brew the coffee. The old adage that "coffee boiled is coffee spoiled" still held true. It is wise to keep a careful count of the cooking time. (4) Keep coffee utensils absolutely sweet and clean."

Daily washing and weekly scouring were essential. For further directions in coffee making, Mary Dunbar indicated that the reader look in "Mary Dunbar's Cook Book". In closing, she recommended one round or two level tablespoons of coffee per cup of water for a full-strength beverage.

Mary Dunbar asked readers to join the Home Service staff in making the 1930 New Year's Resolution — to serve excellent coffee every time! That would mean so much to the rest of the meal!

During 1930, the Jewel corporation, along with the Brazilian-American Coffee Committee, presented the Coffee Matinee. It was a program of sparkling music and entertainment. Their message was to learn why coffee is America's favorite drink. The broadcast was aired each Thursday from 5:00 to 5:30 PM, E.S.T., or 4:00 to 4:30 PM, C.S.T., and Tuesday, 5:00 to 5:30 P.S.T., on one of the following stations: WJZ, New York; WBZ, Springfield; WBZA, Boston; WHAM, Rochester; KDKA, Pittsburgh; WLW, Cincinnati; WENR, Chicago; KWK, St. Louis; KFAB, Lincoln; WREN, Kansas City; KGO, San Francisco and KECA, Los Angeles.

In 1938, the question was ask — why is Jewel's triple-cut grind an all-purpose grind, ideal for brewing coffee in any good coffee maker? In order to answer that question, a coffee man must know first that an ideal brew of coffee is one containing the proper amount of coffee, along with the proper amount of aroma and flavor-giving coffee oils. An ideal brew is also a brew free from undesirable flavors and practically free from sediment. Jewel's grind produced this ideal brew because it combined the best kept and extracted qualities.

In order to keep coffee fresh, extract the coffee's fine flavor and aroma, and at the same time extract the maximum number of cups per pound, a grind must consist of given proportions of various size granules. Jewel's portions of the different sizes in a pound of Jewel Coffee are those which have been found best in exhaustive tests by Jewel's New York laboratories and by the Homemakers' Institute.

In order to get a better picture of Jewel's grind, suppose that you put 500 granules of Jewel coffee into your coffee maker when you prepare your breakfast coffee. Just one out of those 500 granules would be the coarsest granule found in Jewel Coffee. Of the next coarsest granules, 120 granules. 59% of the 500 granules, or 295 of them, would be 60 granules. In other words, the five sizes in Jewel's grind are present in these proportions; .2%, 4.8%, 24%, 59%, and 12%. These figures read from coarse to very fine.

It was Jewel's experience and from the findings of many other coffee experts that Jewel's grind produced the maximum number of cups of the finest coffee. They felt that a grind containing a greater proportion of coarse granules would be wasteful, since the customer would have to use more coffee to get a satisfactory cup and no one would enjoy wastefulness? A grind containing more finely ground coffee would grow stale and rancid very rapidly, because the coffee cells would be broken and let the aroma and flavor escape. Even if more finely ground coffee were used immediately after grinding, it would not be satisfactory. Extracting too much of the ingredients from the grounds bring out undesirable elements in the coffee. Tests show that Jewel Coffee with a triple-cut grind made in a Jewel Coffee Maker will produce 96% of all the desirable coffee flavors.

Jewel's modern granulators were scientifically paired steel rollers which cut the coffee beans to the proper sizes. A mixing chamber insures absolute uniformity. Chaff and over-sized granules are automatically drawn off by the granulators. Another modern machine, the True-Flow Bin, insures a correct and uniform flow of the ground coffee from the granulators to the packages.

How did they know that Jewel's grind had just those proportions in every batch, when one pound of coffee contains hundreds of thousands of granules? Impossible as it might seem, Jewel does know that its triple-cut grind never varies. The mechanical operation of Jewel's granulators were checked twice daily by an accurate device called the Ro-Tap machine.

Dated 1939, the above Ro-Tap machine checked the sieve uniformity of ground coffee — scientifically determining its efficiency. Jewel coffee was regularly and carefully tested for customer satisfaction. *Barrington Archives.*

The picture above is Jewel's Ro-Tap machine, which was located in the chief coffee roasters office in Barrington, Illinois. Chief Coffee Roaster Art Hedley, twice a day, took a pound sample of Jewel coffee and put it in the Ro-Tap machine. With a tapping and rotating motion, which never varied in force or duration of time, the machine shook the ground coffee through five screens, one screen placed on top of another.

Each screen retained part of the coffee. When the machine came to a complete stop, Mr. Hedley measured the amount of coffee grains in each screen (on the scales shown in the picture). The scale measures in percentages of the pound sample. If any variation from Jewel's standard grind was shown, the paired rollers in the granulators were immediately adjusted. Modern science and Jewel's devotion to a never-varying standard of quality had contributed to America's coffee enjoyment.

An unknown Jewel employee checks a time ledger of one of the many coffee roasting bins in Barrington. Photograph is dated to the late 1930s. *Barrington Archives.*

The Coffee Expert

The Jewel salesman was a coffee expert. He was trained to answer coffee problems. Customers could choose their coffee maker from the many selections he offered.

For the most complete coffee service in America, Jewel was the answer. For every taste...Jewel offered a blend of coffee to please. Jewel coffees were blended to meet certain taste standards. There was nothing like a good cup of Jewel coffee brewed in a Jewel Coffee Maker, one of their premium percolators, or a Club Aluminum Coffee Maker! Jewel's selection of coffee makers was unlimited, it is impossible to list every coffee maker Jewel offered.

Shown above is the 5-1/2" long measuring spoon and 7" diameter asbestos hot pad. No marking appears on the aluminum measuring spoon or the hot pad. *Author's Collection.*

The 9-cup size Percolator that started in 1/2 minute, combined charm, efficiency and strength. The manufacturer had provided an unusual value in this aluminum percolator, shown above. The fine perforations of coffee basket and water spreader insured uniform percolation and clear coffee. The wide base prevented tipping. The 11-1/4" high percolator sold for $3.90. It was approved by two nationally known institutes — Jewel Homemakers' Institute and the Good Housekeeping Institute. The Percolator was listed in a 1935 ad and could be older. *Randall Collection.*

In the Jewel laboratory, shown below, an unknown Jewel Chemist performed a scientific experiment with Jewel cleaners in this 1923 photograph. Note the Manning-Bowman Percolator on the counter and the two Jewel products. An artist has retouched this historical photograph; note the heavy work on windows, apothecary jars and the percolator. *Barrington Archives.*

In October 1936 the 8-cup Drip Coffee Maker was introduced. It was pointed out that the lid of the pot did not fit the top of the metal dripper. Many 8-cup coffee makers may vary a fraction in height. This should not be of concern.

In 1934 Jewel offered the complete coffee service shown below, which included a nine-cup coffee server. Introduced as part of a complete set, it included the oval 18-3/4" metal tray, asbestos hot pad, and the old style "Rayed" sugar with lid and creamer. The sugar and creamer match the coffee services of that period. The metal dripper, which was a part of a West Bend coffee pot already included in the line, was sold to fit the 9-cup server. *Author's Collection.*

Improved 8-Cup Coffee Maker Introduced —
Barrington, Illinois October 26, 1936

Another historic step in providing "The Most Complete Coffee Service In American" began when the Jewel man took orders on November 2, 1936. Jewel had introduced the new standard line "Hall China Drip Coffee Maker". The eight cup coffee maker was modernized in appearance and improved for making the perfect coffee, just as Jewel had done in 1932 when they first introduced the first modern drip coffee maker. In 1936 they presented the first open, straight-side dripper.

Jewel pointed out the cover of the Hall China server did not fit the new dripper. The open dripper aids the flow of water and the straight edges were easier to clean. There was no practical need for placing the cover on the dripper while the coffee was being made. This progressive step, exclusive with Jewel, is made because it "simplifies coffee making".

The dripper was finished in SATIN-RAY, which was highly stain resistant. The new eight cup coffee maker was just the right size for everyday use.

Variations

Diversification of many coffee and tea pots, as well as other pieces of china, seem to be flukes and collectors will point this out. Perhaps weather conditions caused the unfired green-ware to "sag", resulting in a slightly different size pot. The placement of the decal on the item was probably due to the perception of the person applying the decals, resulting in decals being placed too high or too low, too far to the right or to the left. This can be seen on many pieces. Many collector's are concerned when pieces are found in this condition. No, you don't have a rare piece!

Whether or not a vent hole appears on the lid of a teapot was up to an employee's discretion. Neither Hall nor Jewel was concerned with quality control. As long as the piece looked nice it passed the test. Gold stripes, decal placement, etc., was rejected only if it was obviously wrong.

Granulators

Providing coffee granulators was another aspect of the Jewel Tea Company. As coffee could be purchased either whole bean or ground, for customers who preferred to grind their own coffee Jewel offered various grinders; they appeared periodically in the Jewel News, Premium catalogs and Jewel catalogs.

Arcade Crystal Coffee Mill

In 1926, the Arcade Crystal Coffee Mill was offered. This Mill could be easily attached to the wall or cabinet. It was always ready for use and never in the way. The coffee was kept clean and free from dust in the glass hopper which held a pound of Jewel coffee at a time. The hopper could be unscrewed to be cleaned. The metal parts were of black enamel. Tablespoon graduations were marked on the glass to insure grinding only the desired amount. An adjustment with a locking device assured a satisfactory grind. Using the famous Arcade Crystal Coffee Mill assured you that the coffee was always fresh, fragrant and full bodied. It was Item No. 733 and sold for $1.65.

Only
$1.65
Profit Sharing
Credits or
Cash

This Arcade Mill Is a Dandy
COFFEE MILL—PREMIUM
Freshly ground coffee each morning is truly a luxury, and no trouble at all with this wall coffee mill. The coffee can be stored in the glass container above. The one below serves as a measuring cup. The grind can be easily adjusted; the mill is easily cleaned, and easily filled.   Item No. $1.65
733.......................................
(Cash or Jewel Profit Sharing Credits)

The original advertisement and captions that appeared in a 1929 Jewel News.

The Granulator/Mill shown below bares the Jewel "T" circle logo, introduced sometime between 1922 and 1933. The handle of this grinder is marked "Frediac Mfg/Co., Freeport, Ill." As with most grinders, this model could be attached to the wall or cabinet. This exceptional glass and metal grinder is not easily found. *Hamilton Collection.*

Be on the lookout for a glass coffee canister that is similar to the above glass section to the Granulator/Mill. This canister also bears the Jewel "T" circle logo.

Jewel Granulator

In 1940 the Jewel Premium Catalog offered the electric Jewel granulator, the newest coffee aid for the home. The granulator gave you fresh-ground coffee every time. Listed as Item No. C-6445 and sold for $4.95.

On the inside of the brown lid in the above photograph are the instructions and care of Model J-1. The Grind Adjustments says to keep your coffee in the mill and grind only the amount needed for immediate use. *Hedges Collection.*

The instructions gave a grind adjustment, telling you to loosen the two clamp screws, give two turns, then tighten the screws again.

Coffee Deflector — the hinged gate or deflector controled the flow of ground coffee and prevented a separation of the light and heavy part, thus keeping it uniform. It also instructed one to keep the lid on when grinding. When the motor sounded like it is slowing down, the user was to release the deflector and the coffee would then flow into the glass in a well-blended, even stream.

The label on the granulator reads: JEWEL GRANULATOR - The Most Complete Coffee Service in America, Jewel Tea Co., Inc.

The Jewel granulator was made for Jewel Tea Co., Inc. Barrington, Ill. by the Hobart Manufacturing Co. Troy, Ohio.

In 1940 Jewel promoted the easy-to-use Arcade Coffee Mill. The one-pound capacity glass canister; steel grinding wheel; glass measure for ground coffee. The mill was modern in design; easy to attach and gave the very maximum of flavor from ground coffee. Jewel listed the mill as Item No. 851 and sold it for $2.50. *Hamilton Collection.*

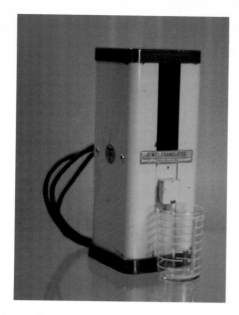

The Jewel granulator shown above with original glass measuring receiver. *Pomroy Collection.*

In 1941 the housewife could take her choice of either coffee granulators, an electric or a hand granulator (shown at the beginning of this section). Each granulator had a one-pound capacity, which could provide fully ground coffee whenever you desired.

An electric coffee bean granulator with the Autumn Leaf motif on the sides has been discovered. Records do not indicate that this grinder ever appeared in any catalog. If any reader has this Autumn Leaf granulator in their collection, I would appreciate hearing from you.

Jewel Coffee Dispenser

During the onset of World War II, Jewel offered a glass dripper. This new glass dripper was built to fit the Hall China Coffee Server, No. 308-A. The pattern of the server matched the other pieces of Autumn dinnerware. The asbestos pad was included with this server. It was a sure way to have good coffee. Metal was scarce and glass could very well be the answer.

If you should have this glass dripper in your collection, I would appreciate hearing from you.

In order to bring out the maximum flavor, yet use less than the usual amount of coffee to brew a cup of normal strength, and also to implement the government's request to conserve coffee and to eliminate the use of metal, Jewel introduced, in 1942, the Hall All-China five-cup capacity maker, No. 325, shown above. It was the first reference made to the pattern by name, exclusively Autumn Pattern. *Byerly Collection.*

In 1941 the first Jewel Autumn Leaf pattern coffee dispenser appeared. It was a combination canister and dispenser, listed as Item No. 6470 and sold for $2.25. The dispenser on the left attached easily to any wall or cabinet and allowed the housewife to notice the amount of unused coffee by viewing the side window of the container. *Byerly Collection.*

The above photograph shows two styles of china inserts. Also note the variation of the decals. *Fausset Photograph.*

Shown above, the three sections of the All-China. It is believed the tall insert was the first to be offered with the All-China. Customers found that they broke easily and it is believed they were restyled to the smaller insert. *Byerly Collection.*

In 1949 the Jewel salesman had a coffee maker for every method of coffee making — drip, vacuum, percolator — glass, aluminum, stainless steel, and ovenware. The Jewel salesman was trained to solve any coffee problem.

The selection of coffee makers in 1949 included: Mary Dunbar Drip coffee maker, 8-cup DeLuxe Vaculator, Favo-Perk Coffee Percolator, and Flavo-Drip coffee marker. A 48-cup DeLuxe Electric Coffee Urn was available for restaurants, churches, or wherever a large quantity of coffee was needed. Additionally, there were the Club Aluminum Drip coffee maker, Hall Drip coffee maker, Mirro Aluminum Percolator, Stainless Steel Coffee Percolator, Silex Lox-in Glass Filter and a Dutch Clothless coffee filter.

Many Jewel salesmen had numerous restaurants, organizations and church accounts where they delivered coffee and tea products where large coffee makers were required.

Introduced in 1957 and selling for $19.95, the 8-cup modern design electric percolator, shown above, was completely automatic. It switched to warm heat after brewing and kept coffee hot for hours. After adding the desired amount of cold water and coffee, the electric percolator did the rest. A safety catch on top prevented the lid from falling off when coffee was served. The electric percolator had a one-year guarantee for defects in materials and workmanship. By 1961 the price had increased to $21.95. In 1969 the selling price was listed as $34.95; during 1969 the electric percolator was discontinued. *Byerly Collection.*

The above original advertisement appeared in the Jewel Home Shopping Service Spring and Summer 1958 Catalog. Note the Club Coffee Dispenser Item (K), also the price of Item (E) has been lowered and penciled in at $14.95.

In a 1972 Jewel Spring and Summer Catalog "LIVE IT UP ELECTRI-CALLY" was highly advertised, with the offer of a variety of coffeemakers, shown below, in the original ad.

BREW DELICIOUS COFFEE

Item (H) was a West Bend 9-cup automatic coffeemaker that brewed delicious coffee automatically. A control kept the coffee hot. The coffeemaker was of polished aluminum with stay-cool handles.

Item (J) was a Landy Vanity 13-cup stainless steel coffeemaker that offered a flavor selector with an automatic signal light. Two thermostats were included — one to brew, one to keep coffee hot.

Item (K) was a 30-cup automatic coffee urn of durable polypropylene that does not absorb taste or odors. It was easy to clean and signaled when the coffee was ready; the self-closing faucet simplified serving and opened with a touch. Offered in Harvest Gold or Flame.

Item (L) was an 8-cup automatic polypropylene coffeemaker that resisted scratching, denting or breaking. It had a flavor selector and indicator light to signal when coffee's ready to serve. It was offered in Avocado, Harvest Gold or Flame colors.

Item (M) was a 10-cup Proctor-Silex automatic coffeemaker. The glass bowl was removable for washing. The coffeemaker had a flavor control.

Item (N) was a Mary Dunbar 9-cup immersible coffeemaker. It was easy to clean, had a seamless stainless steel body, signal lights when coffee's ready, and stayed hot. It also had a black stay-cool handle and base.

Item (P) is a G.E. 9-cup automatic coffeemaker that is immersible. It had a flavor selector, peek-a-brew gauge, chrome plated body with color trims in Avocado, Harvest Gold or Black.

Teapots

"Let's put the kettle on and have a nice cup of tea."

Grown, picked and cured as only the Orient can do with their centuries old experience, Jewel Teas are next brought to this country, cleaned and packaged. The traditions of the ancient, combined with modern science, give you tea perfection. 1931, Jewel News

Tea at its best was selected tea brewed in a Jewel china pot. There were five blends of Jewel Tea — each the finest of its kind available anywhere.

In 1924, No. 329 - Hall's 7-cup green Boston teapot was available. Tea never was so delicious as when brewed in an earthen pot. The pot of graceful lines was beautifully finished fireproof china, and white porcelain lined. A delightful piece of pottery made by the largest manufacturers of teapots in America. This teapot was priced at $1.75 (P.S.C. or cash). This was the first Hall teapot offered by Jewel Tea. *Hamilton Collection.*

The second Hall teapot offered appeared in 1928 as Item No. 330, priced at $1.55. Made of vitrified china, it would not stain, absorb odor, or craze. The lining was of white porcelain. This unique shape and popular olive green color was a winner with Jewel customer's. It was well balanced, easy to pour, and had a 7-cup capacity. While this was the second Hall teapot, it was the third Hall piece offered by the Jewel Tea Co. This Hall teapot would later appear as the Newport Teapot. *Hamilton Collection.*

The Newport is one of the most sought after Autumn Leaf pieces of the teapot line. First, carefully examine your old 1933 Newport teapot! The original Newport that first appeared in a couple issues of the Jewel News of 1933 showed on the lid a small Autumn Leaf motif and the gold was different. Shortly after this motif ceased to appear on the lid and the gold detail changed. A number of collector's believe this may have been a promotional piece.

In the 1933 No. 9 issue of the Jewel News, the caption under the teapot read: "Smartly decorated — There is true delight in making and serving tea with this stunning, vitrified china Hall teapot. The ivory background gives a smart finish to the shades of orange and brown decoration. 7-cup capacity, Item No. 331 $1.50."

Take a look at the steam holes on the lid of your Newport teapots. The older ones have the hole to the side of the final, the newer ones has the hole to the front of the final. Many collectors are concerned with this matter of the location of the steam hole. It has been pointed out to me that various locations of the steam holes can be found on the original as well as the 1978 re-issue. The person employed in that department at Hall China put the steam hole wherever they felt like putting it. To the side or to the front, the steam hole placement made no difference to them.

The Newport, shown above, was reissued in 1978 with gold on the spout and the decal coloring different from the original 1933. The motif is not as large or vivid and bold as the 1933. On the Newport, shown above, the motif appears near the same coloring as other pieces in the Autumn Leaf line. Now look below at the Newport, shown below, and note the additional pink detail that appears in the motif. This is also a 1978 reissue. The reissued Newport is dated "1978" on the bottom. *Byerly Collection.*

The above 7-cup capacity Autumn Leaf Newport teapot was offered in 1933 for $1.50. The spout has no gold trim and no motif appeared on the lid. Note how bold and vivid the decal appears and how it almost covers the side. *Byerly Collection.*

The above teapot, introduced in 1935, also doubled as a 4-cup coffee server. A 1940 Premium Catalog listed "Tea At It's Best"; it was colorful and attractive with any tea service. The above teapot does not appear in catalogs after 1942. This teapot is often referred to as the Long-Spout teapot. *Author's Collection.*

In 1939 the Jewel News listed, with a photograph, the Hall China Teapot as Item No. 302 and sold it for $1.50. The metal dripper was priced at 85¢ and listed as Item No. 68X. In 1941 it was listed as Item No. 302 and still sold for $1.50. It was also guaranteed against breakage.

The teapot with the 4-cup metal dripper top, shown above, was ideal for small families. This metal dripper is highly sought by collectors and may be expensive. *Byerly Collection.*

The Long-Spout Teapot with glass dripper at the left was seen at an Ohio Antique Show. This all-glass and metal dripper harmonized perfectly with this teapot. This dripper fits this teapot perfectly, and the china lid fits the dripper prefect. No markings appear on the glass/metal drip. This dripper should not be confused with the glass dripper mentioned earlier in this section. The only information I could obtain was that the set was purchased from a collector. As is! *Barnes Collection.*

The 7-cup infuser teapot, shown below, is often referred to as "Aladdin". It had no metal parts and was introduced during the early 1940s but discontinued by 1976. It was equipped with an infuser insert that held the tea leaves and lifted out when the tea was as strong as you liked. *Author's Collection.*

The 4" length infuser, shown above, outside of the Teapot with the lid. *Author's Collection.*

The above sugar and creamer were first introduced in 1934 with the No. 300 coffee service. The sugar and creamer match the shape and style of other pieces in the same period. They were discontinued by 1940. *Author's Collection.*

The above sugar and creamer were introduced in 1940. They were designed to match the Hall China Teapot, Coffee Server or other table pieces. *Author's Collection.*

Introduced in 1936, the above cup and saucer is from the regular dinnerware style. Referred to in the Jewel News as "breakfast cup and saucer", it was discontinued in 1976. *Author's Collection.*

Referred to as St. Denis, the above is often called the "HeMan" style cup and saucer. It was introduced in 1942 and discontinued in 1976. *Byerly Collection.*

The above 6" high Irish Coffee mug was introduced at the same time as the 10-oz. beverage mugs. These mugs allowed you to serve coffee in a new and different way by eliminating the use of saucers; each held 10 ozs. *Byerly Collection.*

The above 10-oz. capacity conic beverage mug let you serve coffee, tea, chocolate, etc. It was introduced in 1966, was discontinued in 1976, and reissued in 1978. *Byerly Collection.*

It is wise to remember that cups are best stored by hanging them on cup hooks, which are available at most hardware stores. Stacking cups inside each other can cause chipping.

At one time Jewel had a collection of over 200 rare coffee cups and saucers in their private collection. Little is known as to the whereabouts of the collection today. In a 1941 Premium Catalog, a small caption appeared by one of three cups and saucers. It did not say that these were Jewel cups. The ad was promoting Jewel, however. Shown on the left, one of Jewel's rare cup and saucers that appeared in this promotional advertisement. The marking on the back of one of the saucers read, "Loubat, New Orleans, LA, CARR CHINA CO Design Patent Pending". *Hamilton Collection.*

By 1930 Jewel indicated that coffee keeps its flavor best in a glass canister tightly fitted with a lid. Jewel offered a large glass canister, which held three pounds either ground or in the bean. The opening was large enough to dip a cup inside for filling. The lid turned on or off with just one small twist. If you should have one in your collection, I would appreciate hearing from you.

The 3-lb. canister introduced in 1935, matched the cake-safe and sold for 50¢. Following the introduction of the 3-lb. canister, the addition of two other canisters were added the following July. The two additional pieces sold for 25¢ and 35¢. This completed the three piece canister set, shown above. The set became a casualty of the war and was discontinued by 1942. *Byerly Collection.*

Not until 1959 did another canister set appear with the famous Autumn Leaf motif. The above four-piece square set appeared in the 1959 catalog. This canister set kept sugar, flour, tea and coffee fresh beneath white plastic lids. *Byerly Collection.*

The recessed handle allowed for easy stacking. The canisters could be placed side by side or stacked in various ways. Many of the handles came off after repeated use, as shown above. *Author's Collection.*

In 1960 the new Autumn Coppertone pattern canister set appeared. They were chip-resistant with a baked-on enamel finish and with snug-fitting Coppertone finished lids. The finials were black plastic.

The incomplete Coppertone canister set is shown above. The sugar and flour held 5 lbs. each and the coffee and tea held 1-1/2 lbs. each. *Hamilton Collection.*

Shown above, the 30-cup Jewel Best Coffee Urn. This coffee urn was a salesman award in the late 1970s. *Byerly Collection.*

A set of four china Jewel Best Coffee mugs are shown above. These mugs are quite fragile. Check them thoroughly for any sign of repair. *Hamilton Collection.*

There are numerous commemorative mugs/cups and saucers that can be found in the secondary market. It may take some time in searching this out.

Shown above a set of four commemorative coffee mugs. Each mug displayed a different Jewel coffee. *Randall Collection.*

The above exceptional Jewel Best Coffee advertisement is ©1927. No other information is known about this advertisement. *Hedges Collection.*

CHAPTER 8
CAMEO ROSE

Cameo Rose, an E-style dinnerware pattern made exclusively by Hall China Company of East Liverpool, Ohio for the Jewel Tea Company. The E-line or style dinnerware was popular during the 1940s - 1950s and designed by J. Palin Thorley. This style of dinnerware was produced for Sears, but other non-Sears pieces were produced using a number of different motif decorations. This Cameo Rose dinnerware was first offered in 1951 and remained available until the early 1970s. The pattern features a single white rose, framed by rosebuds and leaf wreath, with gold accent.

This pattern is slowly growing in popularity among collectors, but will never rank in the category of the Autumn Leaf. The green Cameo Rose backstamp is shown below. *Pero Photograph*

A listing from the Jewel Spring and Summer 1952 Home Shopping Service Catalog states: "Of all dinnerware, semi-porcelain is most widely used because a small investment buys an attractive, smart-looking set suitable for all types of serving. It is durable, practical ware with a hard-fired, non-porous glaze that will not craze."

Jewel offered the three piece Cameo Rose tea set, shown below, that included the 8-cup teapot, sugar, lid, and creamer. The 8-cup teapot and lid measures 6" high and 11" from spout to handle. *Author's Collection.*

In 1953, Cameo Rose was offered in cup and saucer, 6-1/4"
bread and butter plate, 7-1/4" salad plate, 8" pie plate, 9-1/4"
breakfast plate, 10" dinner plate, 11-1/2" small platter, 14-1/4"
large platter, 15-1/2" extra large platter, 5-1/4" fruit dish, 6-1/4"
cereal dish, 8" coupe soup, sugar bowl and cover, creamer, 10-
1/2" oval vegetable dish, vegetable dish and cover, gravy boat, 9"
pickle dish, 8-3/4" round vegetable dish, 5" cream soup, 8-cup
teapot and cover, shown above. Salt and pepper shakers, could be
purchased separately or as a pair.

"Fall and Winter" 1961 Jewel Home Shopping Service catalog lists a
1/4 lb covered butter dish for $2.25, shown below. This very expensive
butter dish is one of the most favorite pieces of the Cameo Rose line and
is hard to find. *Pero Collection.*

In 1954, the 3-tier tidbit tray, shown below, was offered for $3.95. This set required some assembly; like the Autumn Leaf tidbit, the hardware came in a envelope. As with the Autumn Leaf tidbit, reports have come to me indicating a 2-tier. This I personally believe to be a fluke as I have found no proof of Jewel offering a 2-tier. If you can provide proof to me, please contact me. *Author's Collection.*

Shown above is the only Cameo Rose cup and saucer offered in this pattern. Collectors should pay close attention to the handles on these cups when purchasing them. They are quite fragile and many cups handles have been glued or mended. *Author's Collection.*

Shown above, the Cameo Rose Covered Sugar and Creamer. In 1954, the complete sugar bowl set sold for $2.65 and the creamer sold for $1.85. No backstamp appears on this set. *Author's Collection.*

Shown above L - R is the 6-1/4" bread and butter, 7-1/4" salad plate, 8-1/4" pie plate and the 9-1/4" Cameo Rose breakfast plate. *Pero Collection.*

Shown above, the 10" diameter Cameo Rose Dinner Plate. *Author's Collection.*

Shown on the right, the Cameo Rose 11-1/2"
Oval Small Platter. *Author's Collection.*

Shown on the left, the 13-1/4" Oval Large
Cameo Rose Platter. *Preo Collection.*

Shown on the right, the 15-1/2" Oval Extra
Large Cameo Rose Platter. *Preo Collection.*

Shown above, the 5-1/4" diameter Cameo Rose Fruit Dish. *Author's Collection.*

Shown above, the 6-1/4" diameter Cameo Rose Cereal or often referred to as a tab handle soup. This is another highly sought after Cameo Rose piece and can be extremely hard to find. *Lemons Collection.*

Above, the Cameo Rose 5" diameter Soup - Coupe sold for 75¢ in 1954. For many collector's this is one of the most difficult pieces to find in the Cameo Rose pattern. *Lemons Collection.*

Shown above, the 8" diameter Cameo Rose flat soup. Not all of these soup dishes will have the backstamp. *Author's Collection.*

Shown above, the Cameo Rose 10-1/2" oval Vegetable Dish. *Author's Collection.*

Shown above, the 8-3/4" diameter round Cameo Rose Vegetable Dish. *Author's Collection.*

The covered vegetable dish, shown above, measures 10-1/2" wide at the handles, the cover measures 8-1/4" in diameter, the bowl is 8" in diameter with a height of 5-3/4". The lid had been removed from the vegetable dish lid so you may see the rose motif in the center of the dish. *Author's Collection.*

Shown above, the Cameo Rose Gravy Boat and the 9" Pickle dish, used as an underplate for the gravy boat. *Author's Collection.*

The 9" Pickle dish/underplate is shown above. *Author's Collection.*

Shown above, the Cameo Rose 2-1/2" high Salt and Pepper shakers. They have cork stoppers. Many shakers have also been found with rubber stoppers. This is not uncommon as the cork stoppers fell apart after numerous uses and were useless. Many were replaced with the rubber stoppers. *Author's Collection.*

Shown below are one-of-a-kind Cameo Rose pieces never put into production. Some of these pieces were purchased in the Jewel employee
outlet store.

A clock from the 10" Cameo Rose Dinner Plate, shown top center. The
Covered Round Casserole, shown on the right — we have covered this
casserole in this chapter. The Wings butter dish, shown in the center,
next to the most unusual Cameo Rose piece, a round covered vegetable
dish. Note carefully the flat lid to this exceptional piece and the curved
tab handles on both the lid and dish. It is not known if this exceptional
piece has a backstamp — I forgot to inquire. *Easley Collection.*

Shown above a closer view of this one-of-a-kind Cameo Rose Clock.
Easley Collection.

Shown above, the electric movement of this clock. This clock could be hung on a wall or, by using the wire stand in the back, set on a shelf or mantel much like a Hall Autumn Leaf clock. *Easley Collection.*

Look closely at the lovely Cameo Rose clock shown above. This is not the one-of-a-kind but a reproduction, made from the 10" Cameo Rose plate. This clock has a quartz movement. *Private Collection.*

Little is known about the 1/4-lb. Wings butter dish shown above. A futuristic design by Eva Ziesel, the shape was Hallcraft. Collectors believe this may have been a sales award. This is the third known Cameo Rose Wings butter dish in a private collection. *Lemons Collection.*

It has been reported that a Cameo Rose tablecloth exists. I know nothing of this tablecloth and have never seen one. If you have such a tablecloth in your collection, I would appreciate hearing from you.

218

CHAPTER 9
NATIONAL AUTUMN LEAF
COLLECTORS CLUB (N.A.L.C.C.)

A SPECIAL ANNOUNCEMENT placed in "The Glaze" publication in 1978 reads, "Hall China-Autumn Leaf-Jewel Tea collectors interested in forming an organization are asked to contact: Nancy Brock in Illinois." Mrs. Brock's address was listed with the announcement. Thus began a search for collectors of the famous china.

In 1978, Nancy Brock and Norma Jones Shaughnessey formed the National Autumn Leaf Collectors Club (N.A.L.C.C.). "The purpose of the Club is to broaden the collectors knowledge of Autumn Leaf Dinnerware and to further the enjoyment and pleasure of collection through fellowship."

MADE ESPECIALLY FOR
THE AUTUMN LEAF CLUB
BY
THE HALL CHINA CO.
1990

The first Club piece, shown below, was the "New York Teapot" produced in 1984; a total of 536 teapots were made. *Byerly Collection.*

Club pieces are a project and made especially for them by the Hall China Company, East Liverpool, Ohio. They are carefully marked as shown above. Any money derived from these pieces goes strictly for the benefit of the organization. Any profits go to offset expenses of annual meetings, newsletter printing and anything that the officers agree upon for the good of the organization.

Shown above is the most beautiful, and much sought after, Club piece –
the "Edgewater" vase offered in 1987; 626 vases were produced. *Author's
Collection.*

Shown above, in observation of the Club's tenth anniversary in 1988 —
the Club offered members a pair of unhandled candleholders. *Byerly
Collection.*

220

In 1990, the above three pieces of "Philadelphia" Tea sets were offered and 1,150 sets of them were made. *Byerly Collection.*

In 1991, the above "Tea for Two" set was offered, which consisted of a teapot, hot water pot and tray. *Author's Collection.*

The "Tea for Two", shown above for the variation of the teapots and the groove in the tray. The groove is for placement of each teapot. *Author's Collection.*

Shown above and on the following pages 223-224 are three Hall China Autumn Leaf pieces made especially for the Club and offered in 1991. The 3-1/2 quart Covered Casserole is shown above. *Author's Collection.*

The Doughnut Water Jug, above, was part of the same 1991 offering.
Author's Collection.

Part of the three piece set is the 1991 8 oz. Solo Teapot is shown above. *Author's Collection.*

The above chocolate tumbler was one of four offered in 1991 with two other Club pieces shown on pages 225-226. *Byerly Collection.*

The Baby Ball Jug, shown above, and a French teapot, shown on page 226, were offered in 1991 along with the chocolate tumblers. The Club distributed 1503 sets. *Byerly Collection.*

A French teapot is shown above. *Byerly Collection.*

Offered late in 1992 and shown above, was a special edition of the Hall Autumn Leaf 8 quart Punch bowl with twelve cups. This has been the largest piece ever offered by the organization. *Author's Collection.*

A novelty "Doughnut" teapot, shown above, measures 10-1/2" from spout to handle and 7-1/2" in height. Offered to Club members in 1993 for the 15th anniversary of the National Autumn Leaf Collectors Club (1978 - 1993). *Byerly Collection.*

Offered in 1984, the above 8-1/2" x 5-1/2" Club cookbook. This was the
first cookbook offered; 500 were printed. Any profits went strictly for
the Club. *Author's Collection.*

The Autumn Leaf Lovers Cookbook

Compiled by Suzan Fausset

A second "Autumn Leaf Lovers Cookbook" shown above was offered in 1991. The 8-1/2" x 6-1/4" cookbook included a collection of member's recipes, pictures of Autumn Leaf China, and many unusual pieces. *Author's Collection.*

For a short time the Club gave members complimentary Christmas gifts. At one time there was a balance in the N.A.L.C.C. treasury, due to a higher estimate of postage made on a Club offer than was needed. The Club decided they would provide an Autumn Leaf sugar packet holder, shown below, for members. The holder was delivered to members around Christmas of 1990. *Author's Collection.*

The fingerhook candleholder, shown below, was sent to Club members for Christmas 1991. *Author's Collection.*

During the 1992 National meeting in Tulsa, Oklahoma, attending members were given a 2" high x 2-1/2" diameter Hall Autumn Leaf Oyster cup with a base measurement of 1-3/4", shown below. There was a total of only 360 oyster cups made. Oyster cups left over were given to members in a drawing during the meeting. Those oyster cups were then mailed to members not attending. The two oyster cups shown below were not free to the attending members; the cost of this piece was included in the registration fee along with the breakfast. It is believed that this has become one of the most sought after pieces ever given by N.A.L.C.C., becoming increasingly more expensive in the secondary market. *Byerly Collection.*

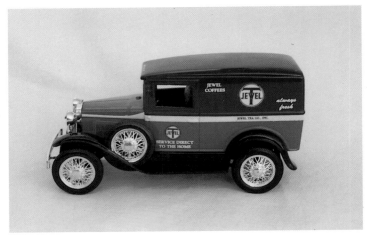

The above bank is a replica of a 1930 Jewel Tea truck offered to N.A.L.C.C. members in late 1993. The truck bank came packaged in a highly decorative and informative container. *Pomroy Collection.*

In a February 1930 "The Jewel News" Vol. 8, No. 2, Jewel introduced "The Jewel Car of Today and Tomorrow." The Jewel News stated "One of the new, clean, efficient, good-looking cars with which the Jewel Tea Co., Inc. is rapidly replacing all of its old equipment. These spic-and-span automobiles give both the Jewel customer and the company a just pride in their appearance, and they give evidence of the effort which the Jewel Tea Co., Inc., makes to bring the best in service to its customer-friends. Cars of this type are the pride of the Ford Motor Comapny's commercial car family." A photograph of the new 1930s Jewel delivery truck accompanied this article along with the statement "In two shades of Brown" in the 1930 Jewel News. Many collectors seek this issue to accompany the N.A.L.C.C. 1930 replica Jewel Tea truck bank.

During Spring 1994, club members received a 3-1/4" Autumn Leaf Bud Vase, compliment of N.A.L.C.C. This piece is well marked and dated 1994. Photograph not available.

New Club pieces are announced in the N.A.L.C.C. newsletter, which is mailed out in January, March, May, July, September and November. All Club pieces were never offered by the Jewel Tea Company; they are manufactured by The Hall China Company, East Liverpool, Ohio.

Anyone interested in joining the N.A.L.C.C. may contact the author through the Publisher of this book. Or refer to Appendix 1 in the back of this publication. Please enclosed a self-addressed stamped envelope for replies.

CHAPTER 10
CHINA SPECIALTIES

China Specialties, Inc. of Strongsville, Ohio started in business in 1986 to market limited edition pottery collectibles. Prior to 1990, China Specialties worked with Homer Laughlin to bring out Fiesta collectibles and Limited Editions.

The President, Virginia Lee Wilson, works closely with representatives of Hall China Co., East Liverpool, Ohio to bring the popular Autumn Leaf back to collectors in limited editions. With the exception of the Airflow Teapot and conic mug, China Specialties Inc. pieces are well marked and dated.

Many China Specialties Inc., pieces will have a gold foil paper label, shown below, and a backstamp.

MARK #1

MARK #2

MARK #3

1992
China Specialties
Exclusive
Limited Edition
by

China Specialties, Inc., backstamps shown above. Mark number 1 appears on the Airflow, number 2 backstamp appears on the conic mug. Some mugs have been found with "Made in the U.S.A" as well as number 2 backstamp.

China Specialties' Autumn Leaf items are in shapes or sizes never decorated with the Autumn Leaf motif before. Virginia Lee Wilson, President of China Specialties, is adamant that these are not reproductions. She says "reproductions are just that...a reproducing of a previously made piece, often to deceive or defraud the collector. The piece is copied line for line, often times even copying the old mark. Our pieces are not reproductions, our items having never been made originally...they are additions to the Autumn Leaf Line, strictly limited in edition, made by the original maker and very collectible in their own right. In addition, we try to pick items that would have been in a residential china service from 1933 to 1978. These pieces have styling characteristics in common with the original line."

China Specialties items are initially offered to their customers at a "pre-introduction discounted price" that approximates wholesale. After a certain percentage of the items are sold, the price begins to escalate. For instance, when the Autumn Leaf Airflow was first offered in June of 1990, it was offered for only $49.95. By October 1990, the price had risen to $59.95. The price continued to escalate until it increased to $150.00 by the end of October 1991. According to Virginia Lee Wilson, such a pricing structure allows China Specialties to achieve a normal profit margin. This still allows the customer who takes advantage of the "early bird" discount to get all their China Specialties' Autumn Leaf items at wholesale and ride the price up. It is truly a win-win situation."

The above "Airflow Teapot" was introduced in 1990 as China Specialties' first Autumn Leaf piece. It was of Art Deco design. Glazed in ivory with 22K gold decoration, it is Hall's most famous shape combined with its most famous decal, a combination that had not existed before. It has proven to be extremely popular. The Airflow teapot was limited to only 1,999 pieces. Unfortunately, this piece is marked in a number of ways. The old Hall in a circle mark might prove confusing for collectors. Toward the end of production, China Specialties and Hall China began to standardize markings and began to date these. However, the majority will not be dated. A few pieces may lack anything but a paper sticker and hang-tag. The price for these has tripled in just two years. *Author's Collection.*

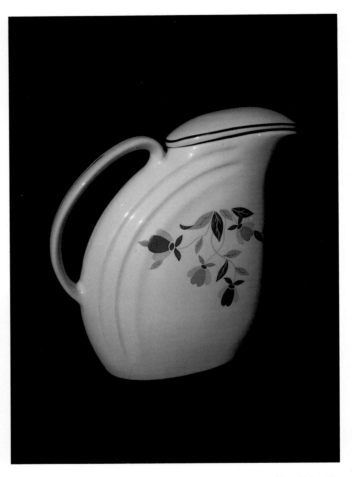

The above "Conic Mugs" were offered in a set of four in late 1990. While they duplicate the shape and decoration of the conic mugs original to the line, the handles were changed to a larger, more comfortable size for practicality as well as to protect the value of each old conic mug. The new type handles suffered problems (breaking off in the Kiln) and were discontinued after 600 sets were made. Hall initially made 17 dozen of the conic mugs for China Specialties using leftover old stock that had originally been made for Jewel Tea. These conic mugs had the original small handle just like the old ones. According to China Specialities, only 12 of these mugs were ever released, and due to the confusion it would cause, there are no plans to release the remaining 16 dozen. The above Conic mug does have a gold seal. *Author's Collection.*

One of the most popular and beautiful pieces introduced by China Specialties is shown above, the "Norris Water Server". Introduced in May 1991, it stands 8-1/4" tall and can be used with or without its loose fitting cover. Holding 48 ounces but only 3-1/2" deep, it is cleverly designed to save space in the refrigerator. It is decorated on both sides with original, old Autumn Leaf Decals that had been in storage. It has gold trim on the lid and handle, and is marked either "HALL 1991", or with mark #3 on the bottom. These were limited to only 1,500 pieces. *Author's Collection.*

The condiment jar shape was designed by Don Schreckengost. While the condiment jar is backstamped, it should be noted that the salt and pepper shakers are not marked. In the secondary market, many dealers have split the set and sold the salt and pepper separately for $250.00 and up. Since the entire three piece set was originally sold for $39.95, the collector should be aware that these shakers are not old and, while they were limited to 1,500 sets, are not worth the hundreds of dollars commonly asked for them in the secondary markets.

An error in marking a few of the condiment sets by Hall China resulted in a recall by China Specialties, Inc. The marking in error read "Made especially for the Autumn Leaf Club (N.A.L.C.C.).

China Specialties, Inc., returned all sets to the Hall China Company in East Liverpool, Ohio for removal of the N.A.L.C.C. backstamp, which was replaced with their own.

The above was a set of four Irish Coffee mugs introduced in August of 1991. While the same height and capacity as the old Irish coffee mugs, these were a more curved, graceful shape. The shape was originally the creation of the noted ceramic designer, Don Schreckengost. The sets were limited to 1,700 and have proven very popular with collectors who have always had a difficult time getting the old original style mugs. These are backstamped two different ways, "HALL 1991" as well as with mark #3. *Author's Collection.*

The above covered onion soups (individual casseroles) were introduced in January of 1992. They were of a shape used in many other decal lines from the 1930s, but never before with Autumn Leaf. The bowls hold 10 ounces and are used at the place setting to serve individual portions of soup or stew. Promotional literature for the item suggested using a single one to hold a tub of margarine on the table. The lid is ivory with gold lining but has no Autumn Leaf decal. These will be found with either the "Hall 1991" or mark #3, indicating they were being produced during both December and January. *Author's Collection.*

The above three piece Condiment set, consisting of a covered condiment jar and "Egg Drop" salt and pepper shakers, was introduced in November, 1991. Patterned after the 1930s "Red Poppy" and "Crocus" which used this shape. The salt and pepper are 2-3/8" high and the condiment jar, holding 5 ounces, is 3-1/2" tall and 3-1/2" across. *Author's Collection.*

The above card party set was one of the more unusual Autumn Leaf pieces made by Hall. Introduced in June of 1992, the scoreboard, shown above, is ivory glazed china. You write directly on the surface with a felt tip marker. To erase, simply wipe the surface with a dry cloth. The Autumn Leaf decal is at the top along with a hole to hang it on the wall. They are backstamped using mark #3 and were limited to 1,200 pieces. The playing cards, shown below, are of linen finish with a metallic gold border and were available in both regular and pinochle decks. They are dated 1991 in white print in the lower right hand corner. *Author's Collection.*

The following *Autumn Leaf Collector's Prayer* was introduced in late 1992. The Hall China Scoreboard Shape (from the card party set) was specially decorated with the original prayer, written in brown lettering and fired on permanently. The prayer was written by Virginia Lee Wilson, President of China Specialties.

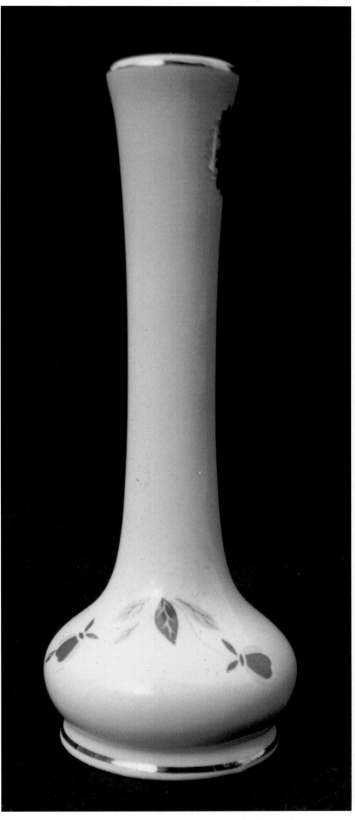

In May 1992, the above limited edition bud vase was well received. This began a new concept — the super limited edition items. Only one was made for each of China Specialties 950 established customers. The bud vase originally sold for $30, and within months began to sell for $125 and up. The vase measures 8-1/8" tall. *Author's Collection.*

In September 1992, China Specialties, Inc., offered the above four, Hall China 2" x 3-7/8" sherbets, which have a low "cushion" foot. These were limited to 1,400 sets, and were offered at the same time as the Libbey Water Goblets, shown elsewhere in this Chapter. *Author's Collection.*

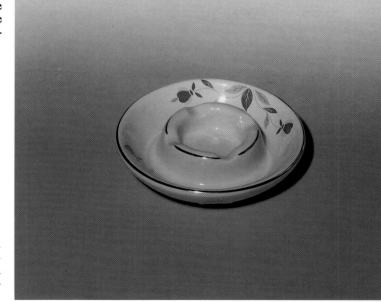

The super-limited Autumn Leaf ashtray on the right was offered by China Specialties, with only one being made for each of their established customers as of November 1992. For non-smokers the ashtray could hold a large 6-1/2" tall pillar candle. The ashtray measures 5-1/2" across by 1-1/2" tall. Only 1,179 ashtrays were made. *Author's Collection.*

The two pieces of stemware, shown below center, was offered in time for Christmas 1992. China Specialties offered 1,500 sets of four Libbey 11 oz. Water Goblets, and a set of four Libbey 8 oz. Wine Goblets. The coloring of the decals on these goblets are a better match than the old "Libbey" or "Brockway", and the glassware was crystal, not frosted. Libbey will no longer frost within 1" of the rim due to lead release concerns.

The Libbey Glass Autumn Leaf Cruet, shown above on the left, was introduced in 1993. The cruet has a 6 ounce capacity, is 4-3/8" in height, and 3" in diameter. Full color Autumn Leaf design on both sides, gold band at the neck. China Specialties offered the cruet in either pairs or single; they were perfect to hold oil and vinegar.

Introduced with a Beer Pitcher was the 6-3/4" tall Libbey Pilsner Glass, shown above—second on the right. The glass hold 15 ounces of beverage and is clear glass with the Autumn Leaf design on both sides and a gold band at the top. The Pilsner glass was limited to 1000 sets of four. Note the wide gold band at the top. This band can be also found narrow.

In 1993 China Specialties offered a set of coordinating Libbey glass juice tumblers, shown above, on the right. Note wide gold band, as with the Pilsner, this also can be found with a narrow band.

China Specialties offered a special Regional Ohio Autumn Leaf "Libbey Shot Glass/Toothpick Holder". This special glass could only be purchased at the Ohio 1993 Show. A single motif appears on the front and on the back appears "OHIO Autumn Leaf Show Columbus, Ohio".

Additional Shoot Glass/Toothpick Holder's, shown above center, could be purchased through China Specialties, these were not marked in regards to the Ohio Regional Convention and a motif appears on both sides. *China Specialties Collection.*

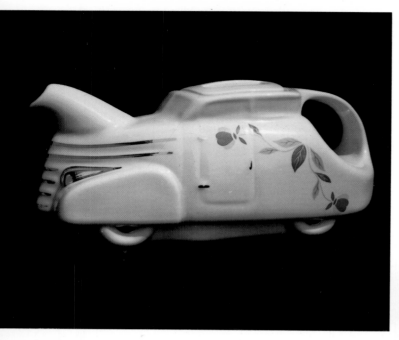

As a tribute to the Jewel Tea Route Salesman, and as a perfect way to celebrate the Gala 60th Anniversary of the Autumn Leaf pattern, China Specialties, Inc. offered the above "Delivery Car" teapot to each of their 1,200 Autumn Leaf customers. It was also offered to each of their established Automobile teapot customers. The teapot holds six cups and measures 9" long and 4" high. It is lavishly decorated with 22K gold trim on the grill, headlights, hubcaps, door handles and hinges, and the Autumn Leaf decal is on both back fenders. In addition, a sprig of Autumn Leaf decorates the handle. Below the handle, a 1933 Illinois license plate with the letters "AUTMNLF" is permanently fired on in brown. *Author's Collection.*

Each Autumn Leaf "Delivery Car" Teapot is numbered on the base of the pot. More importantly, given the importance of the piece, the backstamp reads: "Special 60th Anniversary Commemorative Issue. *Autumn Leaf 1933 to 1993* Produced by THE HALL CHINA COMPANY for the first time in 1933, the Autumn Leaf pattern went on to become the most popular and beloved dinnerware pattern in America. Originally sold door to door and used as premiums by route salesmen of the Jewel Tea Company until 1978, it is now considered one of the top collectibles on the 1990's. A China Specialties Exclusive LIMITED EDITION by HALL."

A Summer announcement was made in 1993 for the new Hall Autumn Leaf Beer Pitcher shown above. The pitcher is approximately 10" tall with a diameter of 5-1/2" and held 80 ounces of your favorite beverage. It is one of Hall's oldest shapes and has a special Limited Edition Autumn Leaf 60th Anniversary backstamp. That reads: "Special 60th Anniversary Autumn Leaf 1933 to 1993, China Specialties exclusive Commemorative Limited Edition by HALL". Less than 1,500 Beer Pitchers were issued. *Author's Collection.*

238

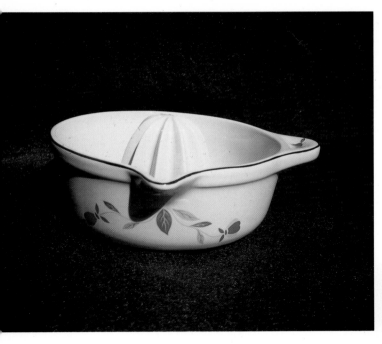

In the Fall of 1993 China Specialties announced the introduction of the Hall China Autumn Leaf orange juice reamer shown above. This reamer was part of the Autumn Leaf pattern's 60th anniversary commemorative line. *Author's Collection.*

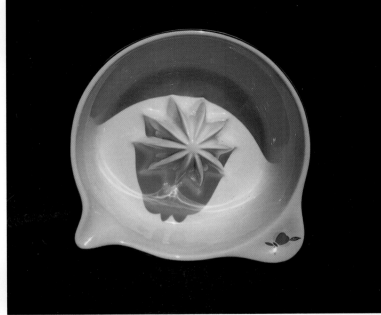

The Autumn Leaf Orange Juice Reamer, shown above, is 7" across to spout. This Reamer was limited to 1,500 pieces and has a "Special 60th Anniversary Hall Backstamp". Note single motif on tab handle. *Author's Collection.*

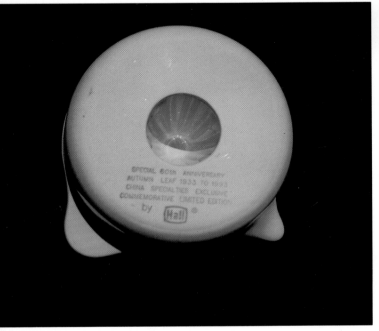

Shown above, the backstamp that appears on the above Autumn Leaf Orange Juice Reamer. *Author's Collection.*

Limited to only 1,550 pieces, the above Autumn Leaf "Baby" one-handle bean pot holds 2-1/2 pints. This is the object of a collector's desire, measuring 5-1/4" tall and 5-1/2" in diameter. *Author's Collection.*

The Oval Handled Relish, shown above, is perfect to hold an assortment of fresh vegetables, olives, and pickles. The Relish Tray measures 10-1/2" x 5-1/2" x 1-1/4" deep. This Tray was limited to 1,500 pieces. *Author's Collection.*

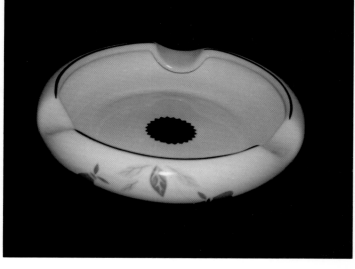

This beautiful round covered Autumn Leaf Butter Dish, shown above, was introduced in the Summer of 1994. This Hall China Autumn Leaf old-fashioned round dome butter dish measures 7-7/8 across, with a 4" tall dome cover. Only 1,599 pieces were made available and sold for $49.95 plus $5.00 shipping. From advanced showings, this butter dish is believed to be the most popular piece offered.

A photograph is not available of a 1994 "Autumn Leaf Calendar Towel". This towel is 13" x 20" in orange, yellow, gold and brown design on natural cotton sailcloth. A limit of 1,000 1994 Autumn Leaf Calendar Towels were available from China Specialties, Inc.

In late 1993, China Specialties provided a sneak preview of the Hall China Autumn Leaf Hurricane Lamp. This 10" tall lamp would be available in 1994. The china base is decorated with the Autumn Leaf motif and gold bands. The clear glass shade has only a gold band. A photograph of this delightful Hall China Hurricane Lamp was not available. Check China Specialties publication's for the introduction of this Hurricane Lamp.

Let's party!. China Specialties offers their established customers first chance to be a China Specialties Party Plan host or hostess. Friends interested in collecting "Hall China" are gathered together. The host or hostess displays the China Specialties items from their collection. Those interested in purchasing China Specialties items fill out their order forms and write checks directly to China Specialties. The host's and hostesses then tally the total points earned on their hostess forms and select their gifts. An example, the hostess earns 12 points for each Airflow or Norris sold or 2 points for each set of four sherbets a guests buys. The guest's order forms and their checks are forward directly to China Specialties and in turn they ship by U.P.S. directly to the guest. All sales are processed just like a regular direct mail order and the prices are the regular retail prices from China Specialties' current flyer. The only difference is that the host/hostess get a special limited issue Autumn Leaf item for bringing China Specialties the sales.

Based on the items they purchase, the party host earn points; with those points the host can purchase items from the regular line or purchase the "special hostess gift" items produced especially for the party plan by Hall China. China Specialties has a second, distinctly different style Hall China Autumn Leaf Ashtray that is limited to 200 pieces available only as a "hostess gift". They also plan to have special Autumn Leaf Libbey Glass items available only to the party plan host or hostess. Periodically their Hall China party plan premiums will change. Shown above this limited addition Cigar Autumn Leaf Ashtray. *Private Collection.*

Note: As of this publication, China Specialities Inc. of Strongsville, Ohio no longer offer their party plan.

The Cigar Autumn Leaf Ashtray "hostess gift" has a foil seal and is also backstamped as shown above. *Private Collection.*

China Specialties, Inc. is pleased to present the above 5-1/2" tall Hall Autumn Leaf St. Louis Chocolate Pot in connection with the publication of this book. Anyone interested in this charming Chocolate Pot may either write China Specialties, Inc. or watch for their forthcoming publication introducing you to this lovely 16 ounce Chocolate Pot. This pot is a companion to the Hall St. Louis Chocolate tumblers (Mugs). See Appendix.

The lid to the Chocolate Pot has been removed. Note gold trim on finial and on lip. This piece will surely add that old fashion touch of charm to cold winter days when steaming hot chocolate is served.

China Specialties publishes "The Autumn Leaf Reissue Association Newsletter". It is an annual publication of the Autumn Leaf Reissue Association, a marketing organization of China Specialties, Inc. Membership in A.L.R.A., is free and automatic with a thirty-five dollar purchase of an Autumn Leaf piece from China Specialties, Inc. They presently have over 3,000 customers.

In 1993, a new premier issue newsletter was offered to China Specialties customers. The newsletter was for collectors of Hall dinnerware patterns, Hall teapots and Hall Kitchenware. Four issues are offered per year.

CHAPTER 11
AUTUMN LEAF CERAMICS

In today's collecting world of Autumn Leaf, many collectors search for the many ceramic pieces produced by various talented artists across the United States. Some of these pieces are demanding high prices in the secondary market. It has been discovered that some of these ceramic pieces have been tampered with after leaving the studio of the individual artist. Many of the backstamps have been filed off. It is wise to become familiar with the artist's style of work, ask questions and if you are still unsure of a piece, it is wise to leave it alone. (See Appendix for listing of artist)

Illinois resident and former N.A.L.C.C. Secretary/Treasurer Carolyn Robbins designed a line of her own Autumn Leaf ceramic pieces during 1981 - 1983. Mrs. Robbins' ceramic Autumn Leaf pieces are sought after by various collectors.

All Mrs. Robbins' pieces were food and drink safe with the Autumn Leaf design under the glaze. All her pieces were trimmed in gold.

The toothpick holder, shown above, measures approximately 2" high x 1-1/2" in diameter. A single motif appears on each side. The backstamp reads, "Handpainted by Robbins 1983 Fowler, Ill". *Author's Collection.*

The handpainted napkin holder, shown above, measures 4-5/8" x 2-3/4" x 4-5/8". This napkin holder is marked with the designer's name, "C. Robbins". *Fausset Collection.*

Robbins also designed a spoon rest, spooner, pie lift, napkin ring, dinner bell, large bowl and pitcher. Also, she designed a large vase and pair of spoons for the Hall China Autumn Leaf mustard and marmalade. I have been unable to locate these pieces.

Shown below is one of the most sought after Robbins pieces, the 2-piece orange juice reamer. The juice reamer is marked APECIV with the word "handpainted". *Moos Collection.*

Robbins designed a four-place child's tea set. This set included a tray, teapot, creamer, sugar, 4 cups, 4 saucers and 4 plates.

There is also a two-place child's tea set that includes a tray, teapot, creamer, sugar, 2 cups, 2 saucers and 2 plates. Robbins' mini tea set has the tray, teapot, creamer, sugar, 2 cups and 2 saucers.

Shown above, Robbins most beautiful and highly sought after hand painted round covered butter dish. *Hancock Collection.*

Shown above, the backstamp of the above butter dish. This underplate is 7" in diameter. *Hancock Collection.*

The above backstamp has become one of the most well-known markings of attractive ceramic Autumn Leaf pieces appearing on the secondary market and in private collections. These pieces are created by a talented Colorado designer, Connie Sipes.

Connie Sipes became interested in ceramics as a hobby. She became serious when it was apparent that some pieces she liked were not included in the Hall Autumn Leaf pattern. Mrs. Sipes and her mother were collectors of the now famous pattern and, in January 1990, Connie began making pieces for herself. Others became interested after seeing her work and asked if she would make items for them as well.

All the pieces Connie was interested in required molds, of which none could be found. With the help of her husband Carl, who has become a constant source of support, Connie produces the molds and greenware which are needed.

It is a seven-step process to make the China, beginning with pouring the piece into the prepared mold. Once dried, this piece called "greenware" must then be cleaned to remove seam marks and imperfections. Next the greenware is fired in a kiln; the heat turns the piece into a bisque form. The bisque is then glazed, which requires several coats of glazing and is then fired again.

Once this form has been produced, the piece is ready for detailing, a process which includes the application of gold trim and decals which have been custom produced to match the original Autumn Leaf colors. A backstamp is applied to the bottom of each piece to identify it as a C & C Collectable Creations.

The final step is to fire it once again in the kiln. Unfortunately this is where most of the losses occur.

Although ceramics started out as a hobby for Mrs. Sipes, it has progressed into a serious labor of love that emanates from her home in Colorado. Yet, when speaking with her, one realizes that she truly enjoys her work and takes extreme pride in her craft.

Shown above is a view of the covered two-piece oval butter dish. The tray is approximately 7-3/4" long and the height is approximately 3" including the cover. *Author's Collection.*

Shown above is Connie Sipes' rolling pin. *Randall Collection.*

Shown on the right is the Autumn Leaf Ceramic Switch Plate cover by Mrs. Sipes, offered in 1992. *Byerly Collection.*

Shown below, a set of cream color (4) Burner Covers For All Electric Ranges, offered in 1992. The Sipes Burner Covers include 2 large 10" size and 2 small 8" size. *Byerly Collection.*

These covers keep burners clean, protecting them from spills and splattered grease. The covers could be used as a trivet or spoon rest when turned upside down. They are dishwasher safe and heat resistant.

SET OF 4
BURNER COVERS
FOR ALL ELECTRIC RANGES
2 LARGE SIZE, 10 INCH • 2 SMALL SIZE, 8 INCH

In 1993, C & C Collectables® worked with International Silver Co. to reproduce the die from the 1958 Autumn pattern silverplate. The International Silver Co., using durable but beautiful stainless steel, recreated this beautiful tableware. It is perfect in detail, matchless in design, balance and exclusively made for, and only sold through, C. & C. Collectables®. The tableware was offered in a 20-piece service for four. All pieces of this tableware are backstamped, "C & C Collectables® 93".

Talented Washington state artist Diana L. Daves created some of the most beautiful ceramic Autumn Leaf pieces made available to collectors in the famous Autumn Leaf motif.

The above exceptional 3-piece soup tureen was made by Diane L. Daves. The underplate and tureen are marked "DD". *Hancock Collection.*

The beautiful pie lift shown above is a Daves
creation. *Hancock Collection.*

The Daves creation, shown on the right, is a
liquid container with a cup that also serves as
a cap or lid. These pieces are not marked.
Hancock Collection.

The above 2-1/2" high x 8-1/4" long planter is backstamped U.S.A. The artist is unknown; it is believed that this was copied from an original piece, then handpainted. *Author's Collection.*

Also unknown is the artist who designed and handpainted the salad set shown above. This is a wooden set approximately 8-1/2" long, painted white with handpainted Autumn Leaf motifs. *Author's Collection.*

250

CHAPTER 12
HAVILAND

November 1927, The JEWEL NEWS suggested "Thanksgiving Festivities Call For The Autumn Leaf Pattern". The colorful Autumn Leaf Pattern in this exquisite, genuine Haviland ware will grace your table on any occasion.

In December 1927, it was referred to as "The Queen of Chinas" and rightly proud was the housewife whose table was graced with genuine Haviland. The 1927 issue pointed out that there were just two pieces of an open line which anyone could buy from the salesman. The two pieces offered were Bread and Butter Plate, Item No. 180-C, and a Salad Bowl, Item No. 180-I.

When several of Chicago's leading high grade china dealers saw the Jewel Tea Company's Autumn Leaf pattern of 1927 in genuine Haviland ware, they said, "Where in the world did you get a hold of that? We've been trying for years to get something like that, but haven't succeeded yet."

Jewel's Haviland was compared with sets selling as high as $190. There was no difference in the china, of course. Both had the clear translucent high luster and uniform texture of all genuine Haviland ware. But in the patterns, there were none under the $190 mark that could compare with Jewel. As Jewel stated, "It is hard for man to improve on nature, and nature's most beautiful coloring is in its leaves in Autumn. The blending of the golden brown, red, and green is perfect."

The growth of the Jewel Tea Company was materially advanced by Haviland China. Haviland China is composed of 50% alumina and 50% feldspar rock, and the glaze is pure feldspar rock. Body and glaze are fired together and vitrified at the terrific temperature of 3280 degrees Fahrenheit. Domestic china and even English china, being composed of lead, borax and sand, can only be fired at much lower temperatures and consequently are not completely vitrified.

The body of Haviland is so hard — through the vitrified process — that, even when chipped, it will never absorb dishwater or grease, or change color.

In 1840 a lady brought a beautiful china cup into the store of David Haviland in New York to be matched. The beauty of the material told him it was not domestic or English. He decided to find out where it was made, as he saw the possibilities of such ware in this country. His search brought him to Limoges, France, and there he started his factories.

It is this firm that David Haviland started in 1840 which is making Jewel Haviland China today in its own factories in Limoges, France. Also it is made from the same kind of clay and involving the same process. It is characteristic of the manner in which Haviland maintains their quality.

Of course, the firm has grown since 1840 until today it is the largest and best equipped of all fine china manufacturers in the world. This notwithstanding the fact that out three complete regiments raised by the Haviland China Company during World War II, only sixteen men survived.

There are, by the way, several off-shoots of the original David Haviland firm; the only one of note being Theodore Haviland, who broke away from the parent organization in 1902 and started a business for himself. His china ware is also of high class and genuine.

How can you distinguish genuine French Haviland China? It has several earmarks which, taken together, never fail:

First — it is translucent. Put your hand behind a plate and hold it up to the light. Your hand is distinctly visible.

Second — "Haviland, France" is stamped in green on the back of every piece of chinaware made by the Haviland China Company. Wherever you see that stamp you know the item is genuinely Haviland China.

Third — "Decorated by Haviland & Company" is also a distinctive mark of genuine Haviland China. Some Haviland, even though genuine, is sold in plain white and the decoration applied in this country. Frequently such decoration does not hold up because of improper firing. Haviland China Company, therefore, put on their stamp "Decorated by Haviland & Company" so no one could be deceived either as to the ware itself or the decoration.

Fourth — A distinguishing feature of all good French china is a slight irregularity and lack of uniformity of the decorations on the different pieces. This is an absolute guarantee that it is hand decorated china — not machine made.

Fifth — All good china contains sand specks. Just as a bit of information, it is almost impossible to make absolutely perfect china. Haviland & Company makes French china as nearly perfect as is possible.

After the pieces are shaped, they are stacked in a sand oven for baking. To stack means pieces are placed in a rack, one piece on top of another, and baked. Any sand or other particles that drop from the roof of the oven during baking will naturally fall only on the piece of china at the top of the pile. The rest of the pieces in the stack are thus mostly protected from falling particles by the top piece of china. Then again, in tier baking like this, there will naturally be a range of temperatures between the top and bottom of the pile. This means that some pieces will be baked at a higher temperature than others, causing a lack of uniformity in the finished product.

Compare this method with the method of baking Haviland ware. Note carefully — each and every piece of *Haviland is baked in a sand oven individually.* There is no stacking of pieces. Every piece is baked under a uniform heat, resulting in finished products that are as nearly uniform as human devices can make them. Every piece naturally contains, because of this individual baking method, some sand specks due to the fact that there is nothing to protect the china from particles dropping from the roof of the oven onto the china during the baking process.

Most fine china manufacturers leave the sand specks as they are, but Haviland & Company has made it a practice to grind them out as far as possible, then cover the ground out spots with a certain solution and refire the piece. This makes the ground out specks almost invisible. *They are guaranteed not to discolor with use;* nor do they, in any way, mar the appearance or wearing qualities of the china. Here then is a decidedly unique feature of Haviland ware and one that will help you quickly to distinguish genuine Haviland from imitations.

Sixth — With good French china, the foot or ridge on which a piece stands (a plate for instance) is unglazed. If you turn a piece of Jewel Haviland upside-down, you will see what I mean. This is another guarantee of individually fired china. It results from grinding off any particles that might cling to the foot when the china is taken off the tripod after baking.

Now, if you will examine a piece of Jewel Haviland, you will notice the two Haviland stamps on the back. Notice also the spray decorations and that these decorations on the same single piece are not located in exactly the same spot. Now hold a piece so a bright light reflects on it at a slant; see the ground-out and refired sand specks? Finally, notice the unglazed foot.

All four distinctive features are there, are they not? Can there be any question as to the genuineness of Jewel Haviland? Positively, NO!

There is one other aspect that should be brought out at this time — that is the matter of selection. By selection, I mean picking over the stock and selecting the pieces the customers want in the sets they are buying. High grade china houses never permit their customers to make selections. The china is sold and delivered as it runs.

The reason for this is that selections have already been made by the pottery manufacturers before the china is shipped. The men who do the selecting have been working in china factories the greater part of their lives and naturally know far more than the average customer about selecting the pieces of china that should be sold and shipped as sets.

It is, therefore, decidedly inconsistent to permit customers to reselect stock which has already been selected by experts. You will bear this in mind when delivering Jewel Haviland to your customers. Of course, cracks, breaks or chips are an altogether different story. These should be taken back from the customers, returned to the branch and set aside. Then replacements may be taken from open stock and given to the customer in the same way as you would in the case of any other Jewel premium which was delivered in a damaged condition.

Jewel Haviland was guaranteed to give satisfaction just as did all their other premiums. In addition, Haviland & Company guaranteed it to be equal to the Haviland regular selection for which Haviland & Company has always been noted, and equal in selection to any French china on the market of a similar grade and decoration. *Jewel Tea Co., Inc. has the exclusive right to the Autumn Spray decoration, No. 24987, in the United States.*

"Here is a startling, practical example of the first of the Three Jewel Ways of Saving, i.e., Immense Purchasing Power. When you consider you are able to offer this wonderful genuine Haviland China to your customers for less than half the price similar sets are being sold for ($76.15 for 107 pieces), you begin to realize what you have. What a jump you have on your competitors; what a service you give to your customers; wnat an incomparable goodwill builder you have at your command."

"It is only natural that your customers should wonder how you can serve them at such a price, but you explain to them that you realize it is (at some time or another) the ambition of every housewife to own a set of Haviland ware. This China is bought in such tremendous quantities in order to give Jewel customers the opportunity to get sets of Haviland. Knowing that, by buying in train-load lots, we could buy at a very low price and sell this treasured China for almost an unheard of low price. Jewel customers understood and thanked their lucky stars they were customers of Jewel. They would, more than ever, appreciate Jewel service. Then they would spread the good news to their friends."
— 1927

Jewel employees were trying, to the best of their ability, to live up to their 1927 slogan "DO EACH JOB BETTER IN '27." It was going to be mighty hard to do a better job than the company had done by getting Haviland in the line — and such fine Haviland. But they were going to keep on plugging away, doing each the job better, and intending to surprise many more prominent Chicago dealers before the year was up, hoping they would say — "Where in the world did you get a hold of that?"

Circa 1920s - 1929 the "Genuine Haviland" shown in this chapter was ready for any table. The china was colorfully decorated with the Autumn Leaf design. It was different than the 1930's Autumn Leaf pattern. Then the Haviland was offered in open stock which enabled a housewife to complete her set.

In August 1929, Maurice A. Karker who was President of Jewel Tea Company from 1924 to 1942, prepared an editorial in which he stated, "Worry never made friends for anybody. And debts make worries. On the contrary, the man or the woman who pays cash has fewer worries than one who has a number of bills and statements hanging over her head."

Purchases for cash meant savings had to be substantial enough to be worthwhile. No prudent buyer could afford to overlook Jewel's savings.

Shown on the left is the Haviland sugar bowl with lid and creamer. Note the 24K gold trim on the handles. *Hancock Collection.*

Shown above is a Haviland round vegetable bowl. *Hancock Collection.*

Shown above is a Haviland 11" small platter. *Hancock Collection.*

Shown above is a 13" round open tab handle serving plate. Note the gold trim on the handles. *Hancock Collection.*

Shown above is a Haviland 9" oval platter. *Hancock Collection.*

Shown above is the Haviland 10" dinner plate. *Hancock Collection.*

Shown above is a Haviland 3-1/4" diameter cup and 5-1/2" diameter saucer. Note the gold trim on the handles. *Hancock Collection.*

Shown above is a 9" Haviland breakfast plate. *Hancock Collection.*

Shown above is a 7" luncheon plate. *Hancock Collection.*

Shown above is a Haviland flat round soup bowl. *Hancock Collection.*

Shown above is a round berry bowl. *Hancock Collection.*

Shown above is a round cereal bowl. *Hancock Collection.*

Shown above is a Haviland 3-piece 24K gold trim 1-lb. round butter dish. *Hancock Collection.*

The Autumn Leaf Haviland China shown in this chapter was only a few pieces from a private collection of approximately 114 pieces, all pieces are in mint condition. This collection also includes a large Haviland covered vegetable bowl with gold on the handles and on the finial of the lid.

The Haviland shown above is stamped "Haviland France Limoges". Jewel's Haviland China also appeared on the covering of a 2-lb. coffee tin and was pictured in various Jewel News articles during the 1920s.

APPENDIX 1

When writing to any of the individuals listed below, enclose a stamped, self-addressed, return envelope, or no reply will be mailed to you in return.

Patti Byerly, Vice President N.A.L.C.C.
4514 Errington Rd.
Columbus, Ohio 43227

Barrington Area Historical Society
Michael J. Harkins, Executive Director
212 West Main Street
Barrington, Illinois 60010

China Specialties, Inc.
19238 Dorchester Circle
Strongsville, Ohio 44136

C. & C. Collectibles
4204 Shelly Avenue
Colorado Springs, Colorado 80910

Shirley Easley (Reprints Jewel Catalogs)
120 West Dowell Road
McHenry, Illinois 60050

Suzan Fausset (Non-Hall Autumn Leaf)
6505 West Cameron
Tulsa, Oklahoma 74127

The Hall China Company
The Hall Closet
East Liverpool, Ohio 43920
Tours: (self guided) Monday through Friday, 9:30 to 2:15.

Hall China Collector Club Newsletter
P.O. Box 360488
Cleveland, Ohio 44136

Opal Hancock (Haviland Autumn Leaf China)
720 Cortez Street
Clewiston, Florida 33440

J&B Antique Mall (Autumn Leaf China)
Jerry and Beverly Nichols, Owners
109 West Adrian Street
Blissfield, Michigan 49228

APPENDIX 2

Common Terms Used by Jewel Men

P.S.C—Profit Sharing Credits.

A Buyer—1) Must make at least one payment in the last 4 trips. 2) Her total payment during the last 4 trips must be $2.00 or 10% of her budget balance, whichever is greater.

Non-Buyer—or delinquent account is an account that does not met the above described standards for a buyer.

New Customer—1) Has received a premium of $2.50 to $10.00 2) Has received a grocery order of at least two different items and has paid for them. (bona fide or "delivered") 3) Has ordered for next time.

Buyer Count—The number of buyers in a book at any particular time or the total number of buyers for all ten route books.

A Prospect—A party on whom you are calling, and hope to make a bona fide customer.

Premium—An item of general merchandise that the customer is paying for through the application of bonus credits.

Bonus Credit—The amount of credit given to a customer on grocery purchases. (example: cream shampoo - $1.00 with 35¢ bonus.)

Budget Merchandise—The General Merchandise a customer has received and is now paying for on regular time payments.

Shipment—The merchandise sent to the Franchise Operator weekly from the Branch or Distribution Center Warehouse.

P.N.C.—Personal New Customer written and delivered by Assistant Manager, Franchise Operator or Manager.

Route Builder New Customer— Written by Route Builder.

APPENDIX 3

Hall Autumn Leaf Backstamps

Shown above, the three Hall backstamps that can be found on the back of the Hall Autumn Leaf pattern. Superior Hall Quality Dinnerware and Hall's Superior Quality Kitchenware, both "Tested and Approved by Mary Dunbar Jewel Homemakers Institute." The 1978 reissue backstamp "Superior Hall Quality Dinnerware. Tested and Approved by Mary Dunbar Jewel 1978". However, there are those pieces of Hall Autumn Leaf that do not have a backstamp.

APPENDIX 4

JEWEL COMPANIES INC. - SALES

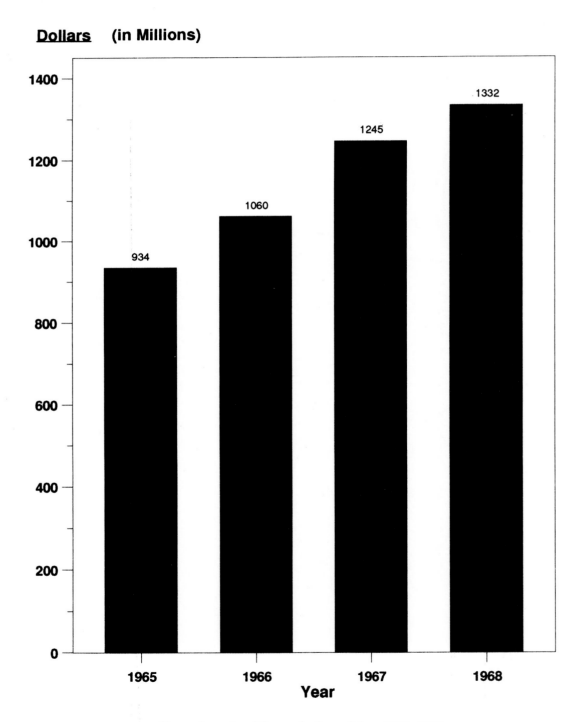

Dollars (in Millions)

Shown above, Jewel Companies Inc., - Sales - 1965 - 1968.

APPENDIX 5

COMPANY CONTRIBUTIONS TO EMPLOYEES RETIREMENT FUND (J.R.E.)

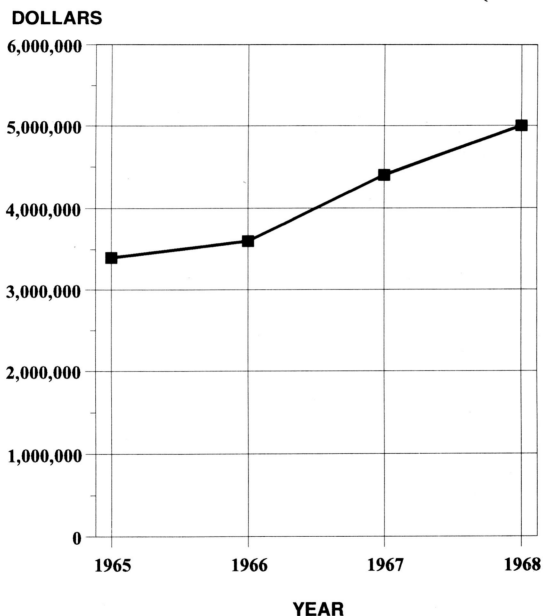

Shown above, Jewel Contributions to Employees Retirement Fund
(J.R.E.), years 1965-1968.

APPENDIX 6

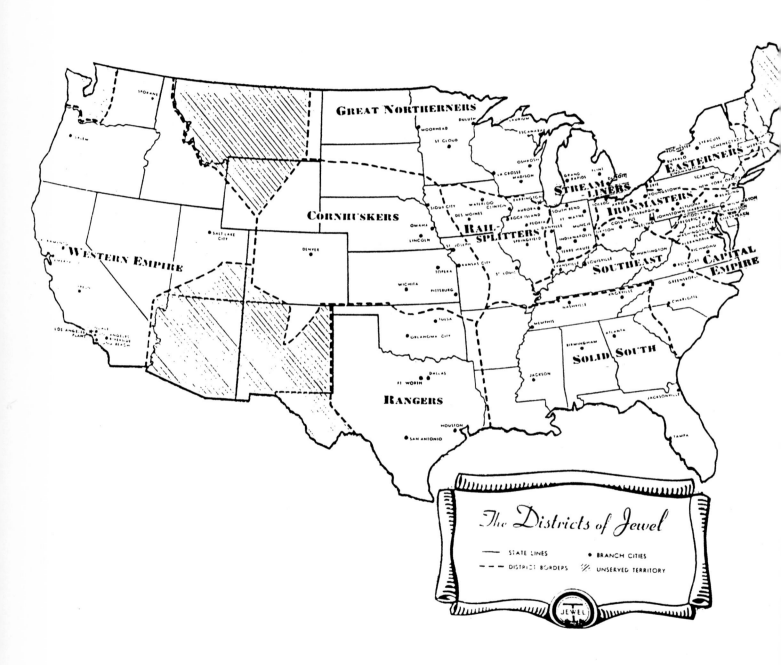

The Districts of Jewel offices and territories served in 1941, shown above.
The Pacific Northwest had just begun, but the outbreak of World War II
hindered that expansion.

BIBLIOGRAPHY

Burness, Tad, *Auto Album.* 1969 Scholastic Book Services New York - Toronto - London - Aucklance - Sydney

China Specialties Inc., Re-issues Newsletter. Virginia Lee, President

Cunningham, Jo, *The Autumn Leaf Story.* 1976 HAF-D Productions

Cunningham, Jo, *The Collector's Encyclopedia of American Dinnerware.* 1982 Collectors Books

Cunningham, Jo, Editor *The Glaze.* March 1977 - September 1985.

Derwich Jenny B. and Dr. Mary Latos, *Dictionary Guide to United States Pottery & Porcelain (10th & 20th Century).*

Disasters. Arno Press New York 1976, Edited by Arleen Keylin and Gene Brown

Duke, Harvey, *Hall 2.* 1985 ELO Books

Jewel News, 1925 - 1948

Jewel Home Shopping Cataloges, 1949 - 1950 - 1960 - 1970.

J.T.'s General Store IHSS, Inc. Jewel Home Shopping Service, Annual Report 1982.

Kovels, *Depression Glass & American Dinnerware.* Fourth Editions. 1991, Crown Publishers, Inc. New York

LIFE. January 13, 1941

Illinois Manufacturers Directory. 1993

Mary Dunbar's Cook Book. ©1927 Jewel Tea Co., Inc., New York Chicago

Mary Dunbar's Favorite Recipes. Jewel Tea Co., Inc. Jewel Park, Barrington, Ill.

Mary Dunbar's Favorite Recipes. Jewel Tea Co., Jewel Park, Barrington, Ill.

Mary Dunbar's New Cook Book. ©1933 Jewel Tea Co., Inc.

Million Dollar Directory. 1992

476 Tested Recipes by Mary Dunbar. Published for and dedicated to the American homemaker by Jewel Tea Co., Inc. Barrington, Illinois.

N.A.L.C.C., Newsletters

Needlecraft, "The Magazine of Home Arts." December 1931

Ohio Manufacturers Directory. 1989 Manfacturers News, Inc.

Oak Leaf. Newspaper January 1947 - March 1947, Oak Park Public Library

Opportunties For Determined Women At Jewel. 1974

Peterson's Guide to Four-Year Colleges. 1990

Schneider, Mike, *The Complete Cookie Jar Book.* 1991 Schiffer Publishing Ltd.

Sharing. Jewel Companies Inc.

The Jewel Cook Book. Jewel Tea Co., Jewel Park, Barrington, Illinois

The Jewel Crusader. 1948 Vol. 7 No. 8 and 1949 Vol. 7 No. 13

The World Book Encyclopedia Edition. 1992

Whitmyer, Margaret & Kenn, *The Collector's Encyclopedia of Hall China.* 1989 Collectors Books

INDEX

A

Advertisement Jewel Best Coffee, 204
Airflow, 232
Aladdin, 196-197
Allspice, 15, 61
American Limoges, 152
Anniversary 75th, 9
Arcade Crystal Mill, 187
Archives Barrington, 59-63, 75, 112-113, 117, 121, 182, 184 185
Asbestos Hot Pad, 185
Ashtray, 236, 241

B

Baby Bean Pot, 240
Bank Jewel Tea Truck, 230
Bean Pot One-handle, 97-98
Bean Pot Two-handle, 99-100
Beck, A.M., 175
Beer Pitcher, 238
Bennett, J.L., 159
Bennighof, Uhl Company, 175
Benson Virginia, 23
Beware, 107-111
Bierman Mrs, 121
Bread Box, 118
Breakfast Cup/Saucer, 198
Breakfast Set, 114
Board Cutting, 117
Boat Gravy AL, 76
Bowl Cereal AL, 81
Bowl Clean, 47
Bowl Salad AL, 84
Bowls Nested AL, 66-67
Blue Jewel, 18-19

Brazilian American Coffee Committee, 183
Brown Mrs., 7
Brown S.H., 159
Brown, W.H., 159
Bud Vase, 235
Buryanek Adeline, 23
Butter Bud One-Pound, 104-105
Butter One-Pound, 100
Butter Quarter-Pound Cameo Rose, 206
Butter Quarter Pound Regular, 100
Butter Quarter-Pound Smooth Top, 102-103
Butter Round Covered, 241
Butter Wings AL, 101-102
Butter Wings Cameo Rose, 218

C

Cake Carrot, 20
Cake Fudge N' Chips, 21
Cake Plate Metal Base, 70
Cake Plate Round AL, 68-69
Cake Rack, 119
Cake Safe, 68, 119-120
Cameo Rose, 8, 205-218
Cameo Rose One-of-a-Kind, 216-218
Candleholder Fingerhook, 230
Candleholders Metal, 70
Candleholders Unhandled NALCC, 220
Candy, 56
Candy Dish Metal Base, 70
Canister Brown Gold white, 137

Canister Coppertone, 202
Canister Round AL, 118, 200
Canister Plastic Lid, 134
Canister Square , 200
Card Party Set, 234
Carroll Leone Rutledge, 121
Casserole Cover AL, 71, 94
Chair Metal AL, 120-121
Cheese Grated, 21
Chicago Plant, 182
China Specialties, 8, 231-242
Chocolate Tumbler NALCC, 224
Cinnamon, 13, 15, 18, 20, 61
Cleanser, 40
Cleanser Can, 122
Cloves, 17, 19
Club Aluminum, 149
Coaster Sets, 127-128
Cocoa, 35-38
Coffee, 27-30, 64
Coffee Dispenser AL, 189
Coffee Makers, 186, 191 -192
Coffee Urn, 203
Collector's Prayer, 235
Columbia, 8, 152, 166-171
Coloring Yellow, 22
Comb Case, 137
Company Hall China, 7
Company Japanese, 8
Condiment Set, 245
Conic Mug, 199, 232
Cookbooks NALCC, 228-229
Cookie Jar Tootsie, 72-74
Cookie Jar Zeisel, 73-74
Cookware, 8, 138-139, 142, 150-151

Corn Flakes, 24-25
Courrier, E.J., 23
Covered Casserole NALCC, 222
Cream Medicated, 46
Cream Whipping, 56
Crooks, G.E., 159
Crooksville, 8, 152, 159-163
Crown, 8, 152, 175-176
Cruet, 237
Cup/Saucer Cameo Rose, 208
Custard Cups AL, 59, 72

D

Daintiflakes, 42
Daves Diana L, 248-249
Delivery Car Teapot, 238
Dish Fruit AL, 81
Dish No. 760, 89
Dreckman, Henry, 23
Dunbar Mary, 9-10, 56, 65, 121, 140-141, 150, 182-183

E

Edgewater Vase, 220
Eggs, 26
Electric Percolator, 191
Extract Lemon, 22-23
Extract Vanilla, 22

F

Factor Condition, 9
Farwell Frank, 23
Fientke, 175
Filling Pudding and Pie, 56
Floral Dresden, 59
Frediac Mfg/Co., 187

French Baker Individual, 90-91
French Baker No. 499, 91
French Baker 2-pint, 90
French Baker 3-pint, 90
French J.M., 159
French Teapot, 225
Fruit Dish Cameo Rose, 211
Frypan Mary Dunbar, 142
Ft. Pitt Baker, 92-93

G

Galloway Mavis, 182
Ginger, 13-16, 18
Glasses Frosted, 75
Glorex, 44
Goddard Julia, 1 21
Grano, 41
Granulator, 188-189
Gravy Boat Cameo Rose, 214
Guarantee, 9-10

H

Hall All-China, 189-190
Harker, 152, 166
Harker Benjamin, 166
Hartson Mary Reed, 7
Haviland, 251-256
Haviland China Company, 251
Haviland David, 251
Haviland Theodore, 251
Heat-Flow Ovenware, 140-141
Hedley, Art, 184
Hembrey Max, 11 5
Hindenburg, 11 5
Hot Pads, 129-131
Hubbard Old Mother, 9-10

I

Illinois Peoria, 175
Irish Coffee, 233
Irish Coffee AL, 199
Ivanhoe, 59, 60

J

Japanese, 179-180
Jeanette Glass Company, 166
Jell, 57, 60, 63
Jetco, 46-47
Jewel Best, 183-184
Jewel Lady, 7
Jewel Rare Cups, 200
Jug Baby Ball, 225
Jug Ball, 74-75
Jug Doughnut Water, 223

K

Kessel Marian, 121

L

Libbey Juice Tumblers, 237
Libbey Pilsner, 237
Libbey Stemware, 237
Lilien K.K., 11 5
Limoges, 8, 172-174
Long-Spout, 194-186

M

Macaroni, 58
Madrid, 60
Manning-Bowman Percolator, 185
Marmalade, 77
Match Holder, 136
Mayonnaise, 59
Measuring Spoon, 185
Meister, Eleanore, 23
Metlox Potteries, 164
Milk Malted, 37-38, 62
Mix Desert, 39
Mix Milk Shake, 36
Mugs Commemorative, 204
Mugs Jewel Best, 203
Mustard, 13-15, 61
Mustard Jar, 77

N

N.A.L.C.C, 8, 219-230
New Jersey Lakehurst, 115
Newport, 193
New York Harbor, 182
New York Teapot, 219
NonHall Unmarked, 176-178
Noodles, 58
Norris Water Server, 232
Nutmeg, 14, 16-17, 61

O

O'Conner Jim, 182
Ohio Regional Convention, 237
Onion Soups, 233
Oyster Cup, 230

P

Paden, 8, 153-158
Paden City, 152
Pads Scouring, 46
Peanut Butter, 59
Peoria Pottery Company, 175
Pepper Black, 13-14, 17, 19, 61
Philadelphia Tea Set, 221
Pickle Dish Cameo Rose, 215
Pitcher Utility AL, 85
Plates AL, 77-80
Plates Cameo Rose, 208-209
Platters AL, 76, 80-81
Platters Cameo Rose, 210
Porcelain Clad Cookware AL, 143-148
Postman, 64
Powder Baking, 10-12
Powder Chili, 20
Powder Soap, 40
Powder Talcum, 44
Poxon China Ltd, 164
Pre-Wash, 47
Punch Bowl, 227

Q

Queen of China The, 251
Quick Chef, 20-21
Quick Oats, 24

R

Range Set, 89
Reamer, 239
Relish, 240
Rice, 26, 31
Robbins Carolyn, 243-245
Ross Frank P, 7
Ro-Tap Machine, 184
Royal Glas-Bake, 143

S

Salem China Company, 172
Satin-Ray, 187
Saucer Breakfast Cup, 87
Schreckengost Don, 233
Sebring China Company, 172
Server Coffee AL, 69
Shakers Cameo Rose, 215
Shakers Casper, 89
Shapira J.M., 61-62
Sherbets, 236
Shuett, Waldo, 23
Sifter Flour, 123
Sipes, Connie, 246-248
Skiff Frank Vernon, 7
Ski-Ro, 16-17
Snack Mix Fruity, 137
Soap Bath, 45
Soup Cream AL, 87
Soap French Process, 43
Soap Pine, 42
Solo Teapot, 224
Soup Cameo Rose, 211-212
Soup Coupe, 86
Spaghetti, 58
St. Denis, 199
St. Louis Chocolate Pot, 242

Stack Set AL, 88
Starch Gloss Lump, 117
Sterling China, 172
Store, JTs General, 8
Story Jewel Coffee, 181-182
Straws, 39
Sugar/Creamer 1934, 186, 197
Sugar/Creamer 1940, 198
Sugar/Creamer Cameo Rose, 208
Sugar Packet Holder, 230

T

Tablets Laundry, 41
Tague A.P., 159
Talbot Mr, 115
Tea, 10, 31-35
Tea Chest, 135
Tea for Two, 221-222
Teapot Cameo Rose, 206
Teapot Doughnut, 227
Teapots, 192-197
Tea Set Cameo Rose, 205
Thermos Picnic, 124-125
Tidbit 2-tier AL, 96
Tidbit 3-tier AL, 95
Tidbit 3-tier Cameo Rose, 207
Tins Fruit Cake, 132-134, 136
Toothpick Holder, 237
Tray Oval Metal, 126, 186
Tray Red, 126

U

Underplate Cameo Rose, 214-215
Unknown, 250

V

Vase Bud, 106
Vegetable Covered AL, 84
Vegetable Covered Cameo Rose, 214
Vegetable Divided AL, 83
Vegetable Oval AL, 83
Vegetable Oval Cameo Rose, 213
Vegetable Round AL, 82
Vegetable Round Cameo Rose, 213
Velvetouch, 40, 45
Vernon Kilns, 8, 164-185
Vernon of California, 152

W

Warmer Oval AL, 93
Warmer Round AL, 93-94
Wastebasket Red, 127
Williams Margaret, 23
Wilson Virginia Lee, 231
Wooden Salad Set, 250
World War II, 116

Z

Ziesel Eva, 73, 101, 218

PRICE GUIDE

Prices vary immensely according to the condition of the piece, the location of the market, and the overall quality of the design and manufacture. Contion is always of paramount importance in assigning a value. The prices in this quide reflect pieces in mint or near mint condition, thouigh the pieces illustrated may not always meet that quality. Prices in the Midwest differ from those in the West or East, and those at specialty antique shows will vary from those at general shows. And, of course, being at the right place at the right time can make all the difference.

All these factors make it impossible to create an absolutely accurate price list, but we can offer a guide. The prices reflect what one could realistically expect to pay at retail or auction.

The left hand number is the page number. The letters following it indicate the position of the photograph on the page: T=top, L=left, TL=top left, TR=top right, C=center, CL=center left, CR=center right, R=right, B=bottom, BL=bottom left, BR=bottom right. The right hand numbers are the estimated price ranges.

11	BR	$50-$65	30	TR	$50-$60	46	B	$20-$25	76	TR	$35-$40 set
12	TL	$35-$45	30	BC	$15-$20	47	TL	$25-$35	76	B	$20-$25
12	TR	$30-$40	31	TL	$50-$60	47	R	$15-$20	77	TL	$60-$75 set
12	CL	$35-$45	31	TR	$50-$60	47	BL	$20-$30	77	TR	$60-$75 set
12	BL	$30-$40	31	CL	$50-$60	48	L	$15-$20	77	B	$10-$14
12	BR	$30-$40	31	BR	$40-$50 ea.	48	TR	$15-$20	78	C	$10-$15
13	TR	$30-$40	32	TL	$10-$15	48	BR	$10-$15	79	C	$10-$12
13	BR	$30-$40	32	TR	$35-$45	49	C	$15-$20	80	TC	(L)$5-$6
14	TC	$30-$40 ea.	32	BC	$20-$25	50	TL	$20-$25			(R)$4-$5
14	BL	$35-$45	33	T	$35-$45	50	TR	$10-$15	80	B	$15-$20
14	BR	$30-$40	33	B	$50-$60	51	C	$8-$12	81	T	$20-$25
15	TL	$30-$40	34	B	$60-$75	52	T	$5-$8	81	B	(L)$4-$5
15	BR	$55-$75 ea.	35	BL	$100+ ea.	52	B	$5-$8			(R)$7-$10
16	TC	$55-$75 ea.	35	TR	$25-$35	53	TL	$20-$25	82	C	$75-$100
16	BL	$50-$75	35	BR	$25-$35	53	BL	$50-$60	83	TR	$75-$100
16	BR	$50-$75	36	TL	$50-$65	55	TR	$65-$75	83	B	$15-$20
17	TL	$50-$75	36	CR	$30-$40	55	BL	$15-$20	84	T	$50-$65
17	TR	$30-$40	36	BL	$50-$65	56	TL	$65-$80	84	B	$15-$20
17	BL	$30-$40	37	TL	$50-$65	56	TR	$100-$125	85	T	$15-$20
18	TL	$30-$40	37	CR	$35-$45	56	BL	$15-$20	86	T	$10-$15
18	CR	$35-$45	37	BL	$50-$65	57	T	$20-$25 ea.	87	T	$25-$30
18	BL	$35-$45	38	TL	$45-$55	57	BL	$25-$35	87	B	$27-$32 set
19	TL	$35-$45	38	BR	$20-$30	57	BR	$15-$20	88	C	$75-$85 set
19	CR	$25-$35	38	CL	$50-$60	ea.			89	T	$35-$40 set
19	BL	$20-$30	39	L	$50-$60	64	BL	$45-$55	89	BL	$20-$25 set
20	TL	$20-$25 ea.	39	R	$5-$10	64	BR	$45-$55	89	BR	$40-$50 set
20	BR	$5-$7	41	BL	$40-$50	66	TL	$30-$35			of 2
21	TL	$5-$7	41	CR	$40-$50	66	B	$50-$75 set	90	T	$14-$18
21	BR	$35-$40	42	TC	$45-$55 ea.	67	T	$50-$75 set	90	BL	$120-$135
22	TR	$50-$60	42	C	$20-$30	68	T	$15-$20	90	BR	$5-$8
22	BL	$50-$75	42	BC	$25-$35	70	T	$150-$175	91	T	$35-$45
22	BR	$30-$40	43	TL	$75-$90	70	BL	$150-$175	92	T	$140-$160
24	BR	$25-$35	43	TR	$75-$90	70	CR	$450-$550	92	B	$140-$160
25	C	$5-$7	43	B	$75-$90 ea.	70	BR	$60-$75 pair	93	TL	$140-$160
26	TC	$40-$50	44	TL	$30-$40	71	T	$25-$35	93	CR	$145-$175
26	BL	$50-$60	44	C	$30-$40	72	TR	$3-$5	93	BL	$100-$120
28	C	$60-$75	44	BL	$25-$35	72	BL	$175-$200	94	T	(T)$25-$35
29	TL	$60-$75	44	BR	$25-$35	73	TR	$175-$200 ea.			(B)$100-
29	TR	$45-$55	45	T	$65-$85	73	B	$175-$200		$120	
29	BL	$45-$55	45	B	$25-$35	74	TL	$175-$200	95	C	$70-$80
29	BR	$45-$55	46	TL	$25-$35	ea.			96	BC	$50-$60
30	TL	$40-$50	46	TR	$20-$25	74	B	$25-$35	97	T	$600-$750

Page	Pos.	Price
98	C	$600-$750
99	C	$160-$180
100	TC	$160-$180 ea.
100	CL	$300-$400
100	CR	$300-$400
100	BC	$175-$200
101	TL	$1000-$1500
101	CR	$1000-$1500 ea.
101	BL	$1000-$1500
102	BC	$600-$700
103	TC	$600-$700
103	BC	$600-$700
104	TC	$2500+
106	TL	$175-$200
107	BR	$25-$30
108	TR	$20-$25
108	BC	$150 set
109	C	$75-$95 set
110	TL	$40-$50
111	C	$65-$75 set
114	BC	$25-$30 4 pc. set
117	CR	UND
117	BL	$75-$100
118	TR	$300-$400
118	BC	$80-$120
119	TR	$50-$75
120	BL	$50-$65
120	TCR	$30-$40
	L	$35-$45
121	TR	$500-$600
122	TL	$800-$1000
122	BR	$800-$1000
123	T	$325-$400
123	BR	$325-$400
124	C	$300-$350
125	TL	$20-$25
126	TR	$75-$100
126	BL	$70-$90
127	T	$300-$350
127	BR	$50-$60
128	BC	$15-$20
129	T	$15-$18
130	BC	$20-$25
131	T	$15-$20 ea.
131	BR	$15-$20 ea.
132	C	$8-$10
133	BC	$10-$15
134	TL	$10-$15
134	BR	$10-$15
135	T	$100-$125
135	B	$15-$20
136	TL	$15-$20
136	B	$10-$15
137	TL	$25-$30
137	CR	$10-$15
137	BR	$25-$35
141	T	$45-$55
141	BR	$25-$30
143	TR	$30-$40
143	CR	$50-$75
143	BL	$50-$75
144	T	$100-$125
144	B	$100-$125
145	T	$60-$70
145	B	$75-$100
146	T	$175-$225
146	B	$175-$225 set
147	T	$175-$225 complete
148	TL	$175-$225 complete
148	BC	$75-$90
149	BC	$75-$100 with original carton/papers
152	BL	$1500-$2000
153	TR	$150-$175
153	BR	$150-$175
154	TL	$150-$175
154	C	$150-$175 ea.
154	BR	$160-$175
155	TL	(L)$160-$175 (R)$175-$190
155	C	$160-$175
155	BR	$175-$195 with original label
156	TL	$155-$170
156	C	$65-$80 ea.
156	BR	$65-$80 ea.
157	TR	$65-$80 ea.
157	C	$500-$600 ea.
157	BL	$850-$1000
158	TR	(L)$350-$450 (R)$450-$500
158	CL	$1500-$2000
158	BR	(L)$150-$200 (R)$200-$275
159	CR	$800-$1000
159	BL	$300-$350
160	TL	$300-$350
160	TR	$200-$250
160	BC	$150-$175
161	TR	$55-$70 ea.
161	CL	$55-$70 ea.
161	BR	$65-$75 ea.
162	TL	$110-$125 set
162	TR	$350-$425
162	CL	$65-$75 ea.
162	BR	$700-$800 set
163	TC	$750-$825
163	C	$750-$825
163	BC	$300-$325
164	T	$800-$1000
164	BL	$150-$165
164	BR	$350-$400
165	TC	(L)$160-$180 (R)$70-$85
165	C	(L)$65-$80 (R)$60-$75
165	BC	(L)$75-$90 (R)$55-$70
166	TL	$1500-$1700
166	TR	$1500-$1700
166	B	$150-$200 ea.
167	TC	$110-$125 set
167	C	(L)$125-$150 (R)$65-$80
167	BC	$65-$80
168	TR	$250-$300
168	CL	(L)$225-$260 (R)$275-$325
168	BR	$250-$275
169	TR	$165-$180
169	CL	$300-$350
169	BR	$800-$900
170	TC	$375-$425 ea.
170	C	$375-$425 ea.
170	BC	$375-$425 ea.
171	TC	$75-$90 ea.
171	C	(L)$250-$275 (M)$250-$275 (R)$275-$325
171	BC	$350-$450 ea
172	BL	$175-$200 set
173	TR	$125-$150 set
173	CL	(L)$160-$180 (R)$85-$110
173	CR	(L)$85-$110 (R)$75-$90
173	BL	$350-$425
174	TL	$700-$800 set
174	C	(L)$375-$425 (R)$375-$425
174	BR	$375-$400
175	CL	(L)$900-$1000 (M)w/lid $650-$750 (R)$650-$750
175	BR	$650-$750 ea.
176	TL	$175-$200
176	TR	$350-$400
176	C	$350-$400
176	BR	$300-$350
177	TL	$300-$350 Pie Lifter $1000-$1200
177	CR	$1000-$1200 ea.
177	BL	$450-$500
177	BR	$300-$350
178	TC	(L)$375-$450 (R)$350-$425
178	C	(L)$500-$575 (M)$500-$575 (R)$475-$525
178	BL	$750-$850
178	BR	(L)$45-$65 (R)$75-$100
179	TL	$150-$175
179	TR	$300-$350
179	BC	$200-$250
180	TC	$300-$350 complete set
180	BL	$200-$250
180	BR	$300-$350
185	CL	Spoon $5-$10 Hot Pad $20-$25
185	TR	$125-$175
186	TL	$30-$40
186	BC	$200 complete set
187	BR	$150-$200
188	CL	$125-$150
188	TR	$100-$125
189	TL	$150-$160 with original measuring glass
189	BL	$250-$350
189	CR	$275-$325
190	T	$275-$325 ea.
190	B	$275-$325
191	TL	$275-$325
192	CR	Green Earthenware 7-cup $25-$35
193	TL	Green Newport 7-cup $30-$40
193	BL	$150-$175
193	TR	$150-$175
193	BR	$150-$175
194	C	$50-$60
195	C	$150-$200
196	TL	$60-$75 with glass drip
196	BC	$40-$50
197	T	$40-$50
197	B	$50-$60 set
198	T	$20-$30 set
198	B	$6-$8 set
199	TL	$25-$30
199	R	$90-$110
199	BL	$50-$60
200	B	$80-$120
201	T	$150-$175
201	B	$20-$25
202	C	$140-$160
203	T	$400-$500
203	B	$25-$30 ea.
204	T	$15-$20 ea.
204	B	$225-$250
205	B	$80-$100 complete 3 pc. set
206	T	$60-$75
206	B	$250-$350
207	C	$50-$60
208	TL	$10-$15 set
208	C	$20-$30 set

No.	Pos.	Price
208	BR	L-R $5-$8, $5-$8, $8-$10, $10-$12
209	C	$10-$15
210	TR	$15-$20
210	CL	$20-$25
210	BR	$25-$30
211	T	$8-$9
211	BL	$15-$25
211	BR	$50-$75
212	C	$10-$15
213	T	$20-$25
213	B	$20-$25
214	T	$50-$60
214	B	$30-$35 set
215	T	$12-$18
215	B	$15-$20 set
216	T	UND
216	B	L-R $50-$60, Wings $250-$300, Covered Vegetable UND
217	C	UND
218	TL	UND
218	CR	$20-$25
218	BL	$250-$300
219	B	$500-$600
220	TL	$275-$300
220	B	$90-$100 ea.
221	T	$200-$250 set
221	B	$150-$175 set
222	T	$150-$175
222	B	$125-$150
223	C	$75-$90
224	TL	$75-$90 set
224	BR	$22-$25 ea.
225	C	$75-$85
226	C	$75-$90
227	T	$300-$400
227	B	$110-$130
228	C	$40-$45
229	C	$25-$35
230	TL	$50-$60
230	CL	$80-$90 ea.
230	TR	$30-$35
230	BL	$250+ ea.
232	TL	$200-$225
232	CR	$150-$175
232	BL	$50-$60
233	TL	$25-$28 ea.
233	CR	$25-$28 ea.
233	BL	$60-$65 complete set
234	T	$35-$38
234	B	$15-$18
235	L	$35-$38
235	R	$100-$125
236	T	$50-$60 complete set
236	BR	$60+
237	C	Cruet $22-$25 Water Goblet $8-$10 ea. Wine Goblet $8-$10 ea. Pilsner $8-$10 ea. Juice $8-$9 Toothpick Holder $5-$8 Ohio Autumn Leaf Show Toothpick Holder $10-$15 not shown
238	TL	$200-$225
238	BR	$70-$80
239	TL	$80-$100
239	CR	$80-$100
239	BL	$80-$100
240	T	$70-$80
240	B	$25-$28
241	TL	$50-$60
241	TR	$125-$130
241	BR	$125-$130
242	TL	$40-$45
242	CR	$40-$45
243	CR	$20-$25
243	B	$30-$35
244	C	$55-$60
245	T	$25-$30
245	B	$25-$30
246	C	$40-$50
246	B	$40-$50
247	TR	$10-$15
247	B	$50-$60 complete set
248	B	$80-$100
249	T	$75-$80
249	BR	$80-$100
250	T	$45-$50
250	B	$50-$75 set
252	BL	$40-$50 set
253	T	$45-$55
253	B	$55-$65
254	T	$55-$65
254	B	$45-$55
255	T	$15-$18
255	BL	$13-$17 set
255	BR	$12-$15
256	TL	$11-$13
256	TR	$12-$16
256	CR	$8-$11
256	BL	$11-$14
256	BR	$70-$80 complete set Gravy Boat with attached underplate $25-$30, not shown. Large covered vegetable bowl not shown, $70-$80

The Jewel Lady